FORBIDDEN FAITH

DEVOTIONS AND INSPIRING STORIES FROM AROUND THE WORLD

GW00342491

CONTRIBUTIONS FROM
JONATHAN AITKEN, LYNDON BOWRING, DAVID COFFEY AND OTHERS
COMPILED BY MERVYN THOMAS, CHRISTIAN SOLIDARITY WORLDWIDE

Copyright © Christian Solidarity International, 2010

Published 2010 by CWR, Waverley Abbey House,
Waverley Lane, Farnham, Surrey GU9 8EP, UK.
Registered Charity No. 294387. Registered Limited Company No. 1990308.

The right of each contributor to be identified as the author of their individual writings
has been asserted in accordance with the Copyright, Designs and Patents Act 1988.

See back of book for list of National Distributors.

Unless otherwise indicated, all Scripture references are from the Holy Bible: New
International Version (NIV), copyright © 1973, 1978, 1984 by the International Bible Society.

Other quotations are marked:

NKJV: *New King James Version*, © 1982, Thomas Nelson Inc.

NASB: New American Standard Bible. Scripture taken from the NEW AMERICAN
STANDARD BIBLE®, copyright © 1960, 1962, 1963, 1968, 1971, 1972, 1973, 1975,
1977, 1995 by the Lockman Foundation. Used by permission.

Concept development, editing, design and production by CWR

Cover image: CWR

Printed in India by Thomson Press Ltd

ISBN: 978-1-85345-548-3

CONTENTS

INTRODUCTION

'Why do good men remain silent? We want you to feel with us in our suffering and cry out when we cannot: "Enough!"'

This call in 1979 by Father Gheorghe Calciu (see page 118) personally stung me into action. It has been the inspiration behind the work of Christian Solidarity Worldwide (CSW) – to be a voice for the voiceless – for over thirty years, coupled with Proverbs 31:8–9: 'Speak up for those who cannot speak for themselves, for the rights of all who are destitute. Speak up and judge fairly; defend the rights of the poor and needy.'

Around the world, millions of individuals face persecution on a daily basis because of their Christian faith. The price they pay can range from discrimination, harassment and imprisonment to torture and even death.

CSW is a Christian human rights organisation specialising in freedom of religion, and our purpose is to be a voice for justice, pursuing religious freedom for all. We document cases of religious persecution, and produce expert reports that are used to influence key decision-makers within the UK and US Governments and the EU and UN, among others. We offer support and solidarity to the persecuted, standing with them in the trials they face. In short, we encourage free Christians everywhere to pray, protest and provide for their persecuted family around the world.

About a year ago as I reflected on the incredible spiritual richness that has personally been imparted to me by so many persecuted Christians over the years, the idea of sharing some of their moving stories with a wider audience was birthed in my heart. I contacted eight of my friends, all with a passion for our persecuted family, and asked them if they would each contribute a week's devotional thoughts to the eight stirring testimonies I had selected. The result was *Forbidden Faith*, a book which I hope will inspire, challenge and motivate you to play your part in raising a voice for our worldwide family. As free Christians we have a responsibility to shout from the rooftops about the gross injustices being perpetrated around the world in this so-called age of tolerance.

Many years ago, a CSW delegation went to Nepal, a Hindu nation, where 130 pastors were imprisoned. At one meeting there, the Police Chief of Kathmandu told our delegation that he was surprised at their visit. He went on to say that he would never dream of imprisoning a Muslim, as the whole of the Islamic world would be up in arms about it. Nor would he think of incarcerating a Jew, as the Jews around the world were so well organised that they would make life very difficult for him. The fact was that until that time he could do what he liked to a Christian and nobody said a word!! When I heard those words, I vowed in my heart that I would do all I could to ensure I never heard them said again, because if there ever is a group of people in the world who should be standing side by side in solidarity, it is the worldwide Body of Christ.

My prayer is that once you have read this book you will be determined to join the ever-growing chorus of voices crying out 'Enough!'

Mervyn Thomas
Chief Executive of Christian Solidarity Worldwide

WEEK ONE
GOD'S MISSION STATEMENT

By Charles Whitehead

AUTHOR PROFILE

Charles Whitehead travels extensively, speaking at local, national and international Christian conferences. For ten years he was President of the Council of the worldwide Charismatic Renewal in the Catholic Church. He is a director of Premier Christian Radio, and writes for a variety of publications. He chairs the International Charismatic Consultation, an ecumenical body promoting co-operation between the churches for world evangelisation in the power of the Holy Spirit, and served as a member of the Azusa Street Centennial Cabinet.

Married to Sue since 1966, they have four children and four grandchildren, and live in Chalfont St Peter, Bucks.

INTRODUCTION

I have enjoyed writing these reflections on Isaiah 61 for a number of reasons. The passage brings sharply into focus the remarkable prophetic ministry of Isaiah, whilst reminding me of the saving mission of Jesus and of the vital work of Christian Solidarity Worldwide (CSW) in our chaotic and frequently unjust world.

Isaiah is one of my favourite Old Testament books because it contains such clear prophecies of the coming of Jesus and of His redeeming work – as we see in the first verses of chapter 61. Then, the fact that Jesus announced the start of His public ministry by quoting these same verses in the synagogue in Nazareth, speaks to me of their special significance, and places their message at the very heart of His mission. The words themselves also remind me of the dignity of every single man and woman created in the image of God, and of their basic human rights to justice and religious freedom, so effectively championed by CSW.

What more could I ask? The missions of my favourite prophet Isaiah, of Jesus my Lord and Saviour and of CSW, whom I support wholeheartedly – all fully present in these inspiring verses of Scripture.

DAY 1

THE PROVISION OF THE HOLY SPIRIT'S ANOINTING

BIBLE READING
Isaiah 61:1–11

KEY VERSE
'The Spirit of the Sovereign LORD is on me, because the LORD has anointed me to preach good news to the poor.' (v.1)

Within the pages of Isaiah we find many of the themes covered in the Old and New Testaments. The prophet presents us with God, the Holy One of Israel, as Redeemer, Saviour and Lord of all. In today's key verse, we are reminded that it is the Spirit of this Sovereign Lord, the Holy Spirit, who anoints Isaiah and inspires all his prophetic utterances. These messages from the Sovereign Lord in Isaiah 61 are just as important for us today as they were for the people to whom Isaiah was directly speaking. God's character does not change. The things which concerned Him hundreds of years ago still concern Him today – *all* His words are everlasting in their importance. So, what we read here is as important for our understanding of God's heart and purposes as it was for the prophet's audience almost 700 years before Christ. There is authority, guidance and power in the Word of God for every age and for every situation.

We, however, have experienced the fulfillment of the Old Testament prophecy foretelling that the Lord would pour out His Spirit on all flesh (Joel 2:28), and since the day of Pentecost all of us who are disciples of Jesus Christ have the Holy Spirit present and active within us, bringing the Word of God alive in our hearts and minds. This is always challenging, but at the same time it gives us both the desire and the ability to put the Word into practice. When God calls, He also enables, and Isaiah's clear reminder that he is speaking under an anointing of the Holy Spirit should cause us to pay particular attention to the words that follow. To give them even more emphasis, Jesus quotes these words in Luke 4:18 as He launches His public ministry.

In a world still troubled by injustice and oppression, such inspired words from Isaiah are a timely reminder of God's concern for those who live in darkness and fear. We need to heed them, for we, too, are called to preach good news to the poor and to proclaim freedom for the captives.

Each day this week, I suggest you meditate on our Bible reading, Isaiah 61:1–11, and each day I will focus on a particular verse from that passage.

PRAYER
Thank You, Lord, for the gift of Your Holy Spirit. Help us to open our hearts and lives more and more to His prompting and guidance.

DAY 2

THE PURPOSE OF THE HOLY SPIRIT'S ANOINTING

BIBLE READING
Isaiah 61:1–11

KEY VERSES
'He has sent me to bind up the broken-hearted, to proclaim freedom for the captives and release from darkness for the prisoners, to proclaim the year of the LORD's favour and the day of vengeance of our God ...' (vv.1–2)

God's anointing is always for *His* purposes, never just for our comfort and enjoyment. The Holy Spirit is concerned with mission – with sending us out. Seven hundred years after Isaiah spoke the words of our passage for this week, Jesus unrolled the scroll in the synagogue in Nazareth and found this prophecy and declared that 'The Spirit of the Lord is on me, because he has anointed me to preach good news to the poor. He has sent me to proclaim freedom for the prisoners and recovery of sight for the blind, to release the oppressed, to proclaim the year of the Lord's favour' (Luke 4:18–19). He stopped short of reading the next phrase found in Isaiah: 'and the day of vengeance of our God'. Why? Because this phrase speaks of His second coming sometime in the future. One day, the year of the Lord's favour will give way to the day of vengeance, as Jesus returns in glory and judgment. In the meantime He has come to speak of God's love and mercy, to demonstrate it by signs and wonders, to establish God's kingdom on the earth, and to give His life so that we may have eternal life.

Today we are still living in the time of the Lord's favour, the age of the Holy Spirit, and we too are sent to announce the kingdom of God. Our mission is to bring the love of God and the freedom Jesus has won for us into every place where there is darkness and oppression. We can only do this because we have the Holy Spirit – not just to help us proclaim the kingdom in words, but to enable us to make it present by our actions. You and I are called to respond to these words of the prophet Isaiah, repeated by Jesus in the synagogue in Nazareth, by taking them seriously and recognising that in our apparently civilised world there are still many who are imprisoned in darkness, lacking that basic freedom which is their right. They need to experience the liberating power of the gospel by encountering Christians who care enough about their lack of freedom to do something about it.

PRAYER
Help us, Lord, to speak out for those who have no voice, to extend a hand to those who cannot help themselves, and to work for the freedom of those unjustly oppressed.

DAY 3

GIVING COMFORT TO THOSE WHO MOURN

BIBLE READING
Isaiah 61:1–11

KEY VERSES
'… to comfort all who mourn, and provide for those who grieve in Zion – to bestow on them a crown of beauty instead of ashes, the oil of gladness instead of mourning, and a garment of praise instead of a spirit of despair.' (vv.2–3)

Grieving helps us to deal with the sense of powerlessness and loss we experience when someone we love suffers or dies. But, in our Western world, mourning is a discreet and rather private affair. Not so in the Middle Eastern world of the prophet Isaiah, where noisy weeping and wailing was the outward sign of mourning that everyone expected. An absence of such loud demonstrations of grief was seen as disrespectful – the louder and more dramatic the signs of grief the better. Professional mourners, usually women, were often hired by a dead person's relatives to weep and wail as the body was carried through the streets. But the verses above tell us that God wants to take away our mourning, grieving and despair, replacing them with blessing, joy and praise. How can this happen?

One of the most frequently asked questions is this: how can a God of love allow suffering? In *The Problem of Pain*, C.S. Lewis writes: 'It is man, not God, who has provided racks, whips, prisons, slavery, guns, bayonets and bombs; it is by human avarice or human stupidity that we have poverty and overwork.' Christians know that suffering is present in the world because of our failure to maintain our original relationship with God, and to carry out the responsibility He gave us to be stewards of His creation. But God is far from indifferent to human suffering. In Isaiah 53:4 we read: 'Surely he took up our infirmities and carried our sorrows ...' Yes, He did, and we know that if the world was living according to the teachings of Jesus, most of the suffering and injustice would disappear overnight. If this is to happen, every Christian has a vital part to play in the social, political, economic and cultural life around them. If a lack of commitment is always unacceptable, our present world situation makes it even more so. No Christian can stand idly by – we all need to get involved.

PRAYER

Lord, show us how to work for change in the world around us, to give people crowns of beauty, to anoint them with the oil of gladness, and to clothe them in the garments of praise.

THE GOD
OF JUSTICE

BIBLE READING
Isaiah 61:1–11

KEY VERSE
'For I, the LORD, love justice; I hate robbery and iniquity.' (v.8)

Justice is important to God, and He sets the standard. Whatever He does is fair, even if we don't fully understand it. This is a major theme in the Old Testament, especially in the Psalms. Knowing how God hates injustice, the psalmists call upon Him to intervene and condemn the wicked, while upholding those who are righteous and just. God's commitment to justice challenges us to examine our own attitudes. Only when we are aware that we have clear obligations towards the wider community, will we look beyond ourselves and begin to seek the common good. As Pope Benedict XVI reminds us in his letter, *Caritas et Veritate* (*Charity and Truth*): 'The development of peoples depends, above all, on a recognition that the human race is a single family working together in true communion, not simply a group of subjects who happen to live side by side.'

When God is accepted and has a place in public life, it is easier to contribute to the development of a just society. The marginalisation of Christianity limits fruitful dialogues between reason and faith, and puts at risk human rights and individual freedoms. As Christians we are called to reveal God's love and to speak God's truth to those around us. To love someone is to want the best for them, and to do everything in our power to realise it. To love the community of which we are a part is to work for its good – politically, economically, culturally, legally and socially. This means putting God in His rightful place in our own lives, irrespective of the attitudes in the society around us. In an increasingly globalised world, our so-called civilised societies have often developed attitudes of self-interest which have inevitably led to the rejection of others, and result in a denial of people's fundamental rights as human beings created in the image of God. When I say I follow a God who tells me 'I, the LORD, love justice; I hate robbery and iniquity', I may need to make sure that society's wrong attitudes have not found a home in me, but that I am committed to loving and working for justice for everyone.

PRAYER

Thank You, Lord, that You are a God of justice and freedom. Guide us by Your Spirit as we try to help those who are denied their basic human rights.

THE GOD OF SALVATION

BIBLE READING
Isaiah 61:1–11

KEY VERSE

'I delight greatly in the LORD; my soul rejoices in my God. For he has clothed me with garments of salvation and arrayed me in a robe of righteousness, as a bridegroom adorns his head like a priest, and as a bride adorns herself with her jewels.' (v.10)

When I first realised what Jesus had done for me through His death and resurrection, and recognised that I could never have done it for myself, I was filled with joy and thankfulness – I was saved! This is what it means to me to be 'clothed with garments of salvation'. Sin's power is no more – I am free to share in God's gift of new life. I don't deserve it and I can't earn it – all I have to do is accept it. But for many people, salvation through faith in Jesus Christ is just too easy – there has to be a catch somewhere. They want to *do* something to save themselves – to please God by their good deeds. Amazingly and wonderfully there's *nothing* we can do – it's a free gift.

To wear new clothes – garments of salvation and a robe of righteousness – is a sign that I am right with God and putting my faith in Him. Just as the bride and bridegroom are dressed in fine clothes and jewellery for their wedding, when I accept Jesus as my Lord and Saviour, He arrays me in the finest clothes and jewels for a great celebration. Christ is now in me and I am in Him, and as I open my heart and life to the Holy Spirit, my inheritance is guaranteed and I am equipped to live this new life of a disciple and a witness. As Paul reminds us in Ephesians 1:13–14: 'Having believed, you were marked in him with a seal, the promised Holy Spirit, who is a deposit guaranteeing our inheritance until the redemption of those who are God's possession – to the praise of his glory.' The call to mission stands at the very heart of the gospel, and so I need to remind myself of the liberating message of salvation in Christ Jesus, and start telling people about it. Because I am anointed with the Holy Spirit, there will be a new love for others in my heart, and I will bring the gospel in word and deed to all who are needy, to all who are suffering or oppressed.

PRAYER

Thank You, Lord, for the gift of new life in Christ. Help me to speak of Jesus to everyone I meet, to be always attentive to the promptings of Your Holy Spirit, and to bring Your love in both word and deed to all who are suffering.

THE STORY OF SISTER LOURDES

When she was just four years old, Maria Lourdes Martins da Cruz listened to her father tell the Nativity story. Born in 1962 into a Catholic family in East Timor, the four-year-old girl was incensed at the injustice surrounding the birth of Jesus. The fact that Mary and Joseph found no room at the inn, and that Mary gave birth in a stable, sparked in the little girl faith, a relationship with Christ and a passion for justice. She went to her own bedroom and prepared a place to receive the baby Jesus, establishing from the very beginning of her walk with God an immediate, deep empathy and compassion for the poor and oppressed.

As she grew up, Maria felt a calling to become a nun. She spent her school holidays assisting priests around the country, and then entered a traditional convent. However, her spirit was restless and she could not settle into convent life. She moved from one religious order to another, unable to find her home. In 1985, when she was twenty-three, her life changed dramatically when God spoke directly to her.

Her country, East Timor, was under brutal occupation. A Portuguese colony for 400 years, East Timor is situated 800 kilometres off the north coast of Australia. In 1975, after the Portuguese withdrew, Indonesia invaded. That invasion came with the tacit approval of the United States and Australia – President Ford and Henry Kissinger were in Jakarta the day before the invasion – and the US and Britain continued to sell arms to the Indonesian occupiers. For the next twenty-four years, Indonesia occupied the half-island. It is estimated that at least a third of the population was killed during the occupation. East

Timorese independence activists were jailed and tortured, women were raped and the entire population terrorised by the Indonesian military. The Catholic Church was at the forefront of the struggle against the occupation. In 1989 East Timor's Bishop Carlos Belo, who later received the Nobel Peace Prize, bravely wrote a cry for help to the UN Secretary General. 'We are dying as a people and a nation', he wrote. It was ten years before he got a response.

Back in 1985, the suffering of her people had deeply affected Maria. She went on retreat and spent several days in almost constant prayer. In front of her was a striking picture of Christ on the cross, the crown of thorns on His head. It was through this image that He spoke to her. After days of weeping and praying, confused as to what she should do to serve God and her people, she heard deep within her a voice: 'I am suffering. What will you do for Me? Why do you spend all your time inside the convent? I do not only live in the convent, I live out there with the poor and the oppressed, and I need you to follow Me there.'

Sister Lourdes
Photo: Christian Solidarity Worldwide 2009

Maria collapsed, unconscious, and when she regained consciousness she knew what she had to do. Sister Lourdes, as she became, founded the Institute of Brothers and Sisters in Christ, her own order, with a specific, radical mission to serve the poor and the oppressed out in the most remote and deprived parts of the country. Replicas of that same picture of Jesus now hang in all the institute's houses around East Timor.

Sister Lourdes, known to many as 'Mana Lou', started the institute with nothing, but gradually a small band of friends joined her and, little by little, with often miraculous provision, they built simple houses for the institute and began ministering to the poor. They became involved in primary healthcare, ministry to the sick, agriculture, education, child care and handicrafts – practical ways of helping the poor with their livelihoods – combined with a passion for justice and freedom, and spirituality.

East Timor's fate changed in 1999, after the fall of Indonesia's long-time dictator Suharto. The new Indonesian President, BJ Habibie, promised the Timorese a referendum, giving them the opportunity to determine their future. However, in the months preceding the ballot the Indonesian military increased its efforts to intimidate the Timorese people. East Timorese militia groups were formed, consisting mainly of ex criminals and thugs. They were paid, drugged and armed by the military, and ordered to terrorise their fellow Timorese into voting to remain part of Indonesia.

Into this escalating crisis stepped Sister Lourdes and her institute, providing vital help and protection to terrified villagers. In April 1999, in Liquica, one of the worst attacks of that year took place. Villagers had sought refuge in the church, believing it was the one place they would be safe. However, militia and Indonesian military threw tear gas into the church, causing everyone to flee outside – where they were gunned down, stabbed and killed. Some hid in the roof of the priest's home, but knowing this, gunmen went in and fired round after round of ammunition into the ceiling until the blood dripped through and they knew everyone there was dead.

In the aftermath of this massacre, most of the local leaders fled. But as they left Liquica towards Dili, they passed Sister Lourdes on her way in, driving through militia roadblocks with food and medicines for the displaced victims of the militia-led carnage. Watched closely by the Indonesians and their militia as she addressed the traumatised villagers, she restricted her speech to spiritual encouragement. According to Dr Daniel Murphy, an American doctor in East Timor, her ability to communicate was extraordinary. Faced with row after row of militia roadblocks, he recalls, she would get out of her car and speak to the militia. 'Within minutes she would have them laughing with her, then crying with her, and then on their knees praying with her.'

Despite efforts by the Indonesian military to intimidate the Timorese into voting for autonomy within greater Indonesia, more than eighty per cent chose independence. They paid a high price for it – within hours of the referendum vote, East Timor was plunged into yet more terror. In the weeks it took the UN to decide how to respond, thousands died and hundreds of thousands were displaced at the hands of the militias. Much of the country's infrastructure was destroyed in an Indonesian 'scorched earth' campaign. Finally, an Australian-led peacekeeping force entered East Timor under UN mandate and restored order. Indonesia withdrew, a transitional government ruled for three years and on 20 May 2002, East Timor became the world's newest nation – and Asia's poorest.

During the worst violence immediately following

the referendum, an estimated 15,000 people fled Dili and sought refuge in the forest around Sister Lourdes house in the mountains above the city. She and the members of her institute looked after the people. 'God worked a miracle,' she said. 'We did not have enough food for even 15 people, let alone 15,000. But each day I got up, I prayed, and then I started cooking rice – and the barrel of rice never ran out for three weeks. The day it ran out was the day the international peacekeepers came.'

Even after the United Nations had come to East Timor, Sister Lourdes' work with the militia and the refugees was not complete. Thousands of East Timorese were still being held by militia in camps in Indonesian-held West Timor and so, in the spring of 2001, Sister Lourdes went there to try to persuade refugees to return home. She went also to help meet their basic physical needs and give them spiritual support.

The camps were still controlled by militia who, she said, wanted to kill her. Each time Sister Lourdes held a meeting with refugees to speak to them about the situation in East Timor and persuade them to return, bare-chested, menacing militia would ride their motorbikes right into the meeting. They would sit inches from her, revving their engines, attempting to intimidate her. She decided to confront the militiamen, but not with fear, anger or hatred. She confronted them with faith. 'Will you come home?' she asked them. 'Will you come home to the Father's house – to God?' As she shared the gospel with them, many of these militiamen – thugs who were guilty of horrific crimes – broke down in tears and converted to Christianity. Those who converted then joined her in her work encouraging the refugees to return home – the very refugees they had been holding hostage.

In 1997, Sister Lourdes was awarded the international Pax Christi Award. Unable to receive it in person, she sent a message that began with these words:

As servants of Christ, we have ideals and dreams. We would like to work with all our strength to build a new world where there will be sisterly and brotherly relations among people. We would like to help them to love one another as true sisters and brothers in Christ.

Sister Lourdes went on to state that 'the people of East Timor live in a situation and atmosphere of suppression' and that their plight was 'a challenge to those who are better off, both inside the country as well as outside, to stretch out a helping hand, to support these people as much as possible'. People could help in different ways, she invited, whether in the fields of development, economics, or politics. 'Political help and attention is important indeed. But the main point is the question: how can we help to lift up the people to human dignity?' Sister Lourdes closed with this thought: 'In all this work we try to co-operate with whoever wants to join us. If we could succeed in this, we would be sure that peace, love, justice, truth, freedom, forgiveness and unity will be born. Peace begins with solidarity.'

WEEK TWO
THE PROMISE OF PERSECUTION

By John Perry

AUTHOR PROFILE

Bishop John Perry is the Deputy Chairman of Christian Solidarity Worldwide (CSW) and also the Executive Chairman of the Lee Abbey Movement. In earlier years, he and his wife Gay were in parish ministry, including St Andrew's Chorleywood, before becoming Warden of the Lee Abbey Community in North Devon. Appointments as Bishop of Southampton and then Bishop of Chelmsford followed. John and Gay have five married children, several of whom are involved in Christian ministry, and a large number of grandchildren.

INTRODUCTION

Several years ago, I read some words by the persecuted Cardinal Kin about suffering which have stayed with me: 'There are many kinds of bread. There is the good, white bread of friendship but there is also the black bread of suffering, loneliness and poverty. This is the bread in which splinters of wood have been mixed. This black bread of suffering should be fraternally divided.' This helped me to understand more fully what it means to belong to the global Body of Christ. The apostle Paul underlined this when he wrote, 'If one part suffers, every part suffers with it …' (1 Cor. 12:26).

To be involved in CSW has opened my eyes, touched my heart and strengthened my resolve to play my part, however small, as a 'voice for the voiceless', for those who are persecuted for their faith in Jesus Christ. Their witness in the face of suffering and loss of liberty is both an inspiration and a humbling, uncomfortable challenge to us in our journey of faith which is woefully incomplete without them. They need us, but how much we need them. The black bread of suffering must be 'fraternally divided'.

WEEK TWO
DAY 1

THE PROMISE OF PERSECUTION FOR FOLLOWING CHRIST

BIBLE READING
John 15:18–27

KEY VERSE

'Remember the words I spoke to you: "No servant is greater than his master." If they persecuted me, they will persecute you also. If they obeyed my teaching, they will obey yours also.' (v.20)

In the verse above, Jesus did not 'beat about the bush'. He was not welcomed in this world. Many people saw Him as a threat to their established order, whether it was religious or political. His life-changing ministry of teaching, preaching and healing was a constant rebuke to the perpetrators of oppression, injustice and exploitation. And He was not slow to expose and challenge religious hypocrisy. Consequently, Jesus was a marked man and had to be eliminated.

As with the Master, so with the follower. The apostle Paul stressed this when writing to Timothy, a young church leader: '... everyone who wants to live a godly life in Christ Jesus will be persecuted ...' (2 Tim. 3:12). The German pastor and theologian Dietrich Bonhoeffer was uncompromising in his opposition to the Nazi regime. This resulted in his imprisonment, danger to his family and finally his execution. Gayle Williams was gunned down in Kabul on her way to work for Serve Afghanistan, a Christian charity that cares for some of the most forgotten people in the world; the poor and the disabled. The Taliban, which claimed responsibility for her killing, blamed her death on her Christian beliefs.

In contrast to many other parts of the world where persecution is on the increase, Christians in the UK rarely face physical attack or abuse. But, as priest and writer Henri Nouwen reminds us: 'We cannot expect always to be liked and admired. We have to be prepared to be rejected.' We should not be surprised when we experience anti-Christian hostility. This may take many different forms. Holding fast to Christian truth and values can sometimes be unpopular, and may even bring discrimination, ridicule or ostracism. The apostle Peter has some helpful advice for those times when opposition is encountered. Read 1 Peter 3:13–18.

PRAYER

Lord Jesus, I pray for all who face persecution for their faith in You. Grant them courage, strength and hope. Thank You for the assurance that 'Blessed are those who are persecuted because of righteousness, for theirs is the kingdom of heaven' (Matt. 5:10). Amen.

DAY 2

THE PROMISE OF BEING DELIVERED TO THE AUTHORITIES FOR FOLLOWING CHRIST

BIBLE READING
Matthew 10:11–18

KEY VERSES
'Be on your guard against men; they will hand you over to the local councils and flog you in their synagogues. On my account you will be brought before governors and kings as witnesses to them and to the Gentiles.' (vv.17–18)

Jesus' warning was soon to be tested by the apostles of the newborn Church in Jerusalem. The Acts of the Apostles chronicles the rapid growth of the Church coupled with mounting persecution of it. This has often been the pattern throughout the history of the Church: spiritual hunger and numerical growth has often stirred up a hornets' nest of persecution. When the light of Christ exposes the darkness of sin and evil, fierce opposition is aroused.

In Acts 4 we find Peter and John hauled before the Sanhedrin after the healing of a crippled beggar and the subsequent response from a large crowd enthralled by Peter's preaching 'Jesus and the resurrection' (v.2). Undeterred by the threats of the Council, the two apostles rejoined the other believers and they said together a remarkable prayer. Read Acts 4:24–31. In Acts chapter 5, the apostles are again in trouble with the authorities, flogged and ordered to stop speaking 'in the name of Jesus' (v.40). But note what happened. Instead of running for cover, they rejoiced that they had been counted worthy to suffer for Christ, and they continued to take every opportunity, whether publicly in the temple courts or from house to house, to share the good news (vv.41–42). This makes humbling reading, as does the account of Stephen's fearless witness before the authorities and his martyrdom. Read Acts 7.

In a world where many Christians are facing persecution and suffering imprisonment, torture and death for their allegiance to Christ, we can feel dwarfed by their faith and courage. But they also encourage us not to be ashamed to confess the faith of Christ crucified and risen. Furthermore, as members of the same Christian family, with prayerful imagination we can 'Remember those in prison as if [we] were their fellow prisoners, and those who are ill-treated as if [we] ourselves were suffering' (Heb. 13:3).

PRAYER

Jesus of the nail-pierced hands, draw near to those who suffer at the cruel hands of oppressive authorities and regimes, and touch them with Your healing love. Amen.

DAY 3

THE PROMISE OF THE HOLY SPIRIT'S PRESENCE DURING DETENTION

BIBLE READING
Matthew 10:19–20

KEY VERSE
'... the Spirit of your Father speaking through you ...' (v.20)

The promise of Jesus that His followers would not be left without the enabling presence and power of the Holy Spirit after His death, resurrection and ascension, was mightily fulfilled at Pentecost and in subsequent experience. The Acts of the Apostles has been described as the Acts of the Holy Spirit, and it is the Spirit who again and again gives wisdom, courage, endurance and inner strength to believers in the face of opposition and persecution.

In days past, a young Christian of wealth and position was being examined by a magistrate and was threatened with severe penalties if he did not renounce his faith.

'I will banish you,' said the magistrate.

'That you cannot do,' replied the Christian, 'for all the world is my Father's house.'

'Very well,' said the magistrate, 'I will confiscate your property and you will be left penniless.'

'That you cannot do,' replied the Christian, 'for my treasure is in heaven.'

'Very well,' was again the magistrate's response. 'I will send you into exile, where you will not have a single friend.'

'That you cannot do,' was the answer, 'for I have a friend from whom you cannot separate me.'

'Enough of this argument,' said the magistrate. 'You shall be put to death.'

'That you cannot do,' came the rejoinder, 'for my life is already given to Christ.'

The apostle Paul gives a vivid summary of his experiences of adversity and persecution in the service of Christ and the gospel: 'We are hard pressed on every side, but not crushed; perplexed, but not in despair; persecuted, but not abandoned; struck down, but not destroyed. We always carry around in our body the death of Jesus, so that the life of Jesus may also be revealed in our body' (2 Cor. 4:8–10). Where did his strength and resilience come from? It was nothing less than the power of the promised Holy Spirit (see 2 Cor. 4:7).

In times of difficulty, uncertainty and pressure, when we may not know what to say in defence of our faith, the Holy Spirit comes to aid us in our weakness.

PRAYER

Come, Holy Spirit, and comfort and empower all who seek your help. May they be given the words to speak and the strength to endure and overcome. Amen.

DAY 4

THE PROMISE OF PERSECUTION TO COME TO THE CHURCH

BIBLE READING
Matthew 10:21–23

KEY VERSE
'All men will hate you because of me, but he who stands firm to the end will be saved.' (v.22)

Jesus presents a solemn picture, when persecution will intensify. Following the martyrdom of Stephen, 'a great persecution broke out against the church at Jerusalem, and all except the apostles were scattered throughout Judea and Samaria' (Acts 8:1). Saul, who had collaborated in the killing of Stephen, was at the forefront of a ferocious attack on the Church. But persecution had the effect, as it often does, of spreading the gospel. Believers were scattered, and Philip, for example, went down to Samaria where a great revival broke out as a result of his preaching and healing ministry (see Acts 8:4–8). And Saul was stopped in his tracks and his life turned upside down when he had a vision of Christ on the road to Damascus. Saul the persecutor became Paul the apostle.

In recent years, the Church in parts of Nigeria has experienced fierce opposition and persecution. Church buildings have been destroyed and Christians killed. Church leaders have been targeted. Ben Kwashi, Archbishop of Jos, and his wife Gloria, have shown immense courage and endurance in the face of unspeakable abuse and torture. They have suffered greatly, yet their confidence in the transforming power of the gospel has remained unshakeable. Archbishop Ben writes, 'The Church will never be killed by persecution, and men of violence will never silence the gospel.'

The apostle John, exiled on the lonely island of Patmos, is reminded by the eternal Christ that the gospel will never be silenced. He is commissioned to write letters from Jesus, both of encouragement and rebuke, to the seven churches in Asia Minor. To the church in Smyrna, soon to suffer persecution, comes the assurance of the Lord's presence and care: 'Be faithful, even to the point of death, and I will give you the crown of life' (Rev. 2:10). To the suffering churches in Nigeria, Orissa in India, Pakistan, Burma, Eritrea, North Korea, Columbia and Cuba, to name but a few, 'the Living One', who is 'alive for ever and ever', brings that same reassuring word of hope (Rev. 1:18).

PRAYER

God of all mercy and grace, I pray for Your Church worldwide facing persecution. May Your perfect love banish fear and may the forces of darkness be overcome by the transforming light of Christ. Amen.

DAY 5

THE PROMISE OF ACKNOWLEDGE-MENT BEFORE THE FATHER

BIBLE READING
Matthew 10:28–33

KEY VERSES
'Whoever acknowledges me before men, I will also acknowledge him before my Father in heaven. But whoever disowns me before men, I will disown him before my Father in heaven.' (vv.32–33)

Accompanying the promise of Jesus in the verses above is a warning. See also Luke 9:25–27. It is undoubtedly true that if there had not been men and women in the Early Church who in the face of intense opposition and persecution refused to deny their faith in Jesus Christ as Lord, the Christian Church would not have survived. And it would not be thriving today in places such as

China and Russia but for the courage of believers down the years who guarded and passed on the gospel to others, often at great cost.

In the parable of the sheep and the goats (Matt. 25:31–46), Jesus leaves us in no doubt that at the Day of Judgment it will be those who have put their faith into action – feeding the hungry, caring for the stranger, visiting the sick and those in prison – who will receive His commendation and welcome. In these acts of faith, Christ is seen and is also ministered to: 'I tell you the truth, whatever you did for one of the least of these brothers of mine, you did for me' (v.40).

By our words, actions or silence, Christ can be acknowledged or disowned. There is an instinctive sympathy for Simon Peter who three times denied knowing his Master when questioned. His numbing sense of failure was eventually put to rest by his encounter with the risen Christ at the sea shore. His threefold reaffirmation of love for his Lord was followed by the commission to care for the flock of Christ. This familiar story not only provides solace and fresh hope to those who falter under the pressures of persecution, but encourages anyone who feels they have failed to hold firm when their faith is under scrutiny by others. No failure need ever be final. Such is the amazing grace and mercy of God.

Hebrews 11 is like a picture gallery, where you are taken around a great hall hung with paintings of men and women of faith, many unnamed. You emerge feeling exhilarated and humbled, especially by those who suffered persecution and untold suffering rather than renounced their faith in God. But you also feel inspired by their example to 'run with perseverance the race marked out for us ... eyes [fixed] on Jesus, the author and perfecter of our faith' (Heb. 12:1–2).

PRAYER

Merciful God, we seek Your forgiveness for when we fall and fail along the way. Lift us up and strengthen us to serve You with renewed faith, inspired by the courageous witness of others for whom we pray. In the name of Jesus. Amen.

THE STORY OF JOEL CRUZ GARCIA

The guerrillas stood around him in the darkness, ridiculing his faith, asking him where his God was. They punctuated their insults by kicking him and beating him with their automatic rifles. One asked him if he was afraid of dying.

In reply, Joel Cruz Garcia, the 27-year-old pastor of a rural Colombian church in the village of El Dorado, lifted his head and quoted Philippians 1:21: 'For to me, to live is Christ and to die is gain.'

The guerrilla leader responded by shooting Joel in the back of the head, execution style.

The FARC guerrillas had come for him earlier in the evening of 5 July 2007. His wife, Yuvy, knew something was amiss by the way the men hammered at the door and the way they did not ask, but rather commanded, Joel to go with them.

The FARC, a Marxist guerrilla group that has been waging war against the government in Colombia for over forty years, continue to maintain a strong presence in many parts of rural Colombia. They are particularly strong in the south, where Joel and Yuvy lived, with their infant daughter.

Although they claim to respect religious freedom, their actions do not support this. FARC defectors have told of a military order that went out in 2002, declaring Protestant pastors to be legitimate military objectives, targeted for assassination. In the parts of the province of Caqueta that they control, they have forcibly shut down all Protestant churches and forbidden Christians from meeting together for prayer or worship.

The rationale for this targeting of Christians, and specifically church leaders, includes the basic conflict between Christianity and the FARC's Marxist ideology; Protestant pastors have reported that the FARC continues to accuse them of being 'agents of imperialism'. There is a more practical reason behind the persecution, however. The FARC relies on complete co-operation from local communities – they regularly use civilians as informants, demand a percentage of income from all local businesses to fund their organisation, expect civilians to work as labourers in the lucrative cocaine trade, and recruit young people, often under duress, into their ranks.

Growing churches in the regions under FARC control are a direct threat to their hold on power. Christian youth refuse to join the guerrilla group, Christian businessmen and women refuse to give money to fund illegal and violent activities, and Christians are reluctant to have any part in the drugs trade. The FARC have understood the power of the gospel to change not only individual lives, but entire

Joel Cruz Garcia's widow Yuvy
Photo: Christian Solidarity Worldwide 2009

communities. Their reaction has been a military one, to target Christian leaders, in particular pastors, for assassination.

The FARC is not the only armed group targeting church leaders. Other leftist groups, like the ELN, as well as right wing paramilitary groups, which operate in much the same way, have reached the same conclusion. The result is that hundreds of pastors and church leaders have been assassinated or have 'disappeared' over the past decade.

The area where Joel pastored was a disputed region, fought over by the FARC, right-wing paramilitary groups and government forces. He was not the only target that evening. Another respected pastor, 63-year-old Humberto Mendez, was murdered by the guerrillas the same night. Two others who worked in neighbouring towns miraculously escaped; one just happened to be away from the town at the time, another was tipped off by someone who knew of the guerrilla's plans, and he fled to the nearest city.

Joel's wife, who was only nineteen years old at the time of his assassination, was left a widow with a nine-month-old daughter. She and her extended family were warned that they should leave the area as quickly as possible, and they fled to the nearest city, where they became part of Colombia's enormous IDP (internally displaced people) population of approximately three million.

In the face of her ordeal and difficult financial situation, Yuvy has not lost her faith. Although at first she said she repeatedly asked God why He had allowed things to happen the way they did, she now says her question has changed to 'For what purpose?' A gifted speaker, she aspires to be a pastor herself.

Despite the best efforts of the armed groups, the murders of pastors have not weakened the Colombian Church. Rather, it continues to grow, particularly in regions hardest hit by the conflict. The case of Joel Cruz Garcia, who spoke words of deep faith even as his life was taken from him, is a clear example. Since his death, the church in El Dorado has grown. This, in turn, has attracted negative attention from the FARC, and many church members have been threatened by the guerrillas. However, they continue to meet and worship God together, standing firm despite the attempts to intimidate them and stop the ministry of the Church.

WEEK THREE
A GREAT CLOUD OF WITNESSES

By David Shearman

AUTHOR PROFILE

David Shearman leads the Christian Centre in Nottingham, a vibrant growing church with around 1,400 members and more than forty nationalities represented.

As well as being passionately committed to the local church, David is well known as a leader of leaders both in the UK and overseas. He is one of the Assemblies of God national leaders in the UK and also serves on the board of Christian Solidarity Worldwide. David has written four books: *The Unstoppable Church*; *Born to Win*; *Twelve Dead Men Speak* and *Hope Against the Odds*.

David is married to Dorothy, and they have two children and four grandchildren.

INTRODUCTION

Life has afforded me the privilege of seeing the world and the Church in many parts of the globe. These experiences have had a profound impact on me, especially the miracle of transformed lives in very different people, places and practices, the courage and tenacity of a multitude of unsung heroes the world over, and the price some pay to attest their faith in Jesus. Combine all this with a growing understanding that one of the important messages that the Hebrew prophets repeated was about justice and the treatment of the poor and the 'stranger', and you get a picture of the compassionate, loving heart of God for humanity.

On this journey I have found that the only way for there to be more of Christ expressed through my life is if there is less of me. The 'dying to self' journey has not been and is still not the most pleasant experience life offers, but its joys and rewards are beyond calculation.

All this inspires my contribution and commitment to Christian Solidarity Worldwide.

DAY 1

THEY CANNOT STOP THE MESSAGE

BIBLE READING
Hebrews 11:32–40

KEY VERSE
'These were all commended for their faith …' (v.39)

I can remember as a boy living in Belfast, Northern Ireland, listening at the meal table to a visiting missionary, home from Africa. He told interesting stories about people, his work for God and, for me as a young boy the most exciting part, his hunting big game. It was sobering some time later to hear that he had been martyred, hacked to death with machetes.

From ancient times, this story

has been repeated countless times on every continent. From Egypt in antiquity – 'the more they were oppressed, the more they multiplied and spread' (Exod. 1:12) – to Ethiopia in the late twentieth century, when Mengistu forced the Church underground and it multiplied astonishingly. It seems a truism that 'the blood of the martyrs is the seed of the church' (Tertulian).

Should we be surprised, when we consider the gilt-edged promise of Jesus Christ who said He would build His Church and the gates of hell would not overcome it (see Matt. 16:18)? A promise made good in every century, including the last one, when, in spite of significant persecution in many places, the Church has seen unprecedented growth to the ends of the earth.

Contrast His prediction with one attributed to Mrs Mao Tse-Tung, that 'the only place to find Christianity in 50 years will be the museum', and you realise whose word you can believe.

Should we then be complacent? Never! In every generation the gospel must be shared. Under persecution should we be paralysed by fear? I don't think so. We must be tenacious in our support of all who lack freedom of religion, who are tortured, abused and even martyred. Will such evil acts halt the spread and power of the message? History says no. We must be bold in our generation to stand with an illustrious column of witnesses, those gone before us and those suffering around us, to proclaim the full power of Christ's good news.

They can try to kill us, but they cannot stop the message.

PRAYER

Lord, I remember all in prison because of their faith and ask Your blessing on all who suffer for the gospel wherever they are. Amen.

DYING TO LIVE

BIBLE READING
Galatians 2:17–21

KEY VERSE
'I have been crucified with Christ and no longer live, but Christ lives in me.' (v.20)

DAY 2

So, the Bible makes it clear, the first will be last, the proud will be resisted by God and the 'man who withholds' will come to poverty. It all sounds so right, it *feels* righteous. Why, then, when we apply the obvious mirror philosophy do most of us find it so difficult? The amazing manifesto of Matthew 5–7, where the 'blessed' are the meek, the merciful and those who mourn, illustrates the idea of an upside-down kingdom. To be full we need to be emptied, to receive we must give, to reach the 'top' we must reach for the 'bottom'.

It is shocking to think that Jesus was happy to be 'late' in arriving at Lazarus' house, knowing his resurrection would be 'for God's glory' (John 11:4). In a world where we live and then die, we must understand that as followers of Jesus we must 'die' before we truly live.

In a postmodern, superficial, 'reality TV' world where many people waste their lives watching others waste theirs, and self-obsession seems to be a pandemic, the call of the Bible to humble ourselves appears to jar or at least to strike a different note. Paul spells it out: 'I have been crucified with Christ and I no longer live, but Christ lives in me. The life I live in the body, I live by faith in the Son of God, who loved me and gave himself for me' (Gal. 2:20).

Viewed one way, it appears that we can live a resurrection life before death and can enjoy a quality of life that should belong to another time and place. Christ lives in me – expressed in Philippians 3:11, 'to attain to the resurrection from the dead'. The verse before sharpens the focus: 'I want to know Christ and the power of his resurrection and the fellowship of sharing in his sufferings, becoming like him in his death ...'

In a world obsessed by success and even appropriate attitudes to purpose and destiny, the deeper notes of the Christian message must not be forgotten; it is in dying that we live or, as one martyr, Jim Elliot, put it, 'He is no fool who gives what he cannot keep to gain what he cannot lose'.

PRAYER

Lord, help me to be less so that in me You can be much more. Amen.

IT WILL COST

DAY 3

BIBLE READING
Luke 9:18–27

KEY VERSE
'For whoever wants to save his life will lose it, but whoever loses his life for me will save it.' (v.24)

In John 6, Jesus begins to make His message clear: following Him carries a cost. The message was somewhat unpalatable. The story reads, 'From this time many of his disciples turned back and no longer followed him' (John 6:66).

Jesus challenged the Twelve about whether they wanted to leave. Simon Peter offered a brilliant reason for staying: "Lord, to whom shall we go? You have the words of eternal life. We believe and know that you are the Holy One of God' (vv.68–69).

In contrast to His expensive message, I find it bizarre the way Western spirituality in modern times can preach such a quick fix, low cost, easy gospel. It is bound to disappoint from every prospect. Jesus made it clear what it looked like to be a true follower: 'If anyone would come after me, he must deny himself and take up his cross daily and follow me' (Luke 9:23). Now that seems reasonably unambiguous.

But should we be surprised? Everything of value has a cost. There are fake bargains on offer like 'gain the whole world' – price, 'lose your soul'. As a friend memorably said, 'People wrapped up in themselves make very small packages!'

Both Old and New Testament teaching make it clear; to become what God intended carries a price tag. Paul in Philippians 2 shows Christ's journey to the high and exalted place and a name above every name. It came via: making Himself nothing, taking the nature of a servant, humbling Himself even to become obedient to death and the cruelty of the cross. It clearly was not an easy journey to the throne of heaven.

Jeremiah uses the illustration of winemaking in chapter 48: '… wine left on its dregs, not poured from one jar to another …' (v.11). The reality of life is that we must leave behind some things that have helped to make us what we are, in order to become what God intended us to be. That pouring process is rarely pleasant but necessary.

As some of our brothers suffer for the faith, let us pay our 'proper' price by daily taking up the cross and becoming the aroma of Christ to our world.

PRAYER
Thank You for the commitment of our Saviour Jesus to pay the full price of our salvation. Help me to be a true follower. Amen.

REMEMBERING IS IMPORTANT

BIBLE READING
Galatians 2:6–10

KEY VERSE
'All they asked was that we should continue to remember the poor, the very thing I was eager to do.' (v.10)

There is a remembering that follows forgetting, but that is not what Paul means in Galatians 2:10 when he summarises the apostles' request, 'All they asked was that we should continue to remember the poor, the very thing I was eager to do'. Here, 'remember' is an active 'call to mind'. It is proactive and intentional behaviour, and Paul's words show his enthusiasm to comply.

Some would say we are

commanded to preach, call it the words of the gospel; others are keen to see miracles, call it the power of the gospel; but Paul understands that without the *actions* of the gospel, the care of the poor and attending to issues of justice, the gospel message is incomplete and lacks its full authenticity.

Paul is only reflecting the words of Jesus from His compelling teaching in Matthew 23–25: 'Then the righteous will answer him, "Lord, when did we see you hungry and feed you, or thirsty and give you something to drink? When did we see you a stranger and invite you in, or needing clothes and clothe you?" … The King will reply, "I tell you the truth, whatever you did for one of the least of these brothers of mine, you did for me"' (25:37–40).

Jesus as a prophet Himself, is restating and echoing the words of the ancient prophets: 'He showed you, O man, what is good. And what does the LORD require of you? To act justly and to love mercy and to walk humbly with your God' (Micah 6:8)!

The true fast that Isaiah explains in chapter 58 includes loosing the chains of injustice … setting the oppressed free … providing the poor wanderer with shelter, and offers in return the promise of God's guidance and strength to all who heed the call.

The work of Christian Solidarity Worldwide and other agencies captures God's heart in its advocacy work. Attending to issues of persecution and the abuse of justice. May God bless the work of such groups and give us all the same heart that cares and makes a difference in our world.

PRAYER
Father, help me to see You in the poor and needy, and may I be Your hands and feet in a broken world. Amen.

THE OTHERS

BIBLE READING
Hebrews 12:1–13

KEY VERSE
'Therefore, since we are surrounded by such a great cloud of witnesses, let us throw off everything that hinders and the sin that so easily entangles, and let us run with perseverance the race marked out for us.' (v.1)

DAY 5

Hebrews speaks of the faith of some of the greats on the Bible landscape. It is good to remind ourselves of their stories. Abraham, who set out not knowing where he was going and many years later having proved the unchanging faithfulness of God, was still prepared to obey when the challenge to sacrifice his son seemed to threaten all his most cherished future dreams. Then we have Noah, who built something that had never been seen to prepare for something that had never happened. That takes faith. What about Moses? At eighty years God calls his name and asks questions. Confused and fearful he obeys anyway. The rest is epoch-making history. These and others stir our faith, challenge our walk and urge us forward in our own obedience.

But there is more to the Hebrews 'list'. Some are simply named: Gideon, Barak, Samson, Jephthah, David, Samuel and the prophets and given a general affirmation (11:32–35). Then the Bible narrative slips into complete anonymity with others. These 'others' were brave and courageous, people of character and principle. They 'were tortured and refused to be released … Some faced jeers and flogging, while still others were chained and put in prison. They were stoned; they were sawn in two; they were put to death by the sword' (vv.35–37).

It is true that Abraham, Noah et al are no more; the heroes of the Bible's history are all gone, the text calls them 'a great cloud of witnesses'. But are the 'others' all gone? I suggest not. The tortured, flogged, chained and murdered 'others' are still paying the price of their faith in many places of the world, and the Bible verdict of such people is still the same: the world is 'not worthy of them' (v.38).

Let us remember, then, to uphold them in prayer and by our actions. Let us seek to live lives worthy of our Saviour Jesus and also of the 'others', our brothers and sisters in Christ who still suffer.

PRAYER

Lord, help me to remember the 'others', those I know and the many I don't. Help me to play my part in Your kingdom and leave this world better for being here. Amen.

THE STORY OF LIONEL AND LALANI JAYASINGHE

Forgiveness, I am sure, is something we all struggle with. The Bible tells us to forgive one another, but where do you find the strength to forgive the person who killed your loved one in cold blood? How do you move forward from your grief without blame, anger or bitterness?

This is how: with joy, faith and courage, all of which radiate from the beaming smile and infectious laughter of Sister Lalani Jayasinghe. Yet behind her joyful spirit is a poignant story of suffering and betrayal.

This is a story from the deep South of Sri Lanka that took place in a village called Tissamaharama. On 25 March 1988, 29-year-old pastor Lionel Jayasinghe was playing with his 11-month-old son while his wife Lalani cooked their simple evening meal. Two men walked into their home and in front of his wife and child shot Lionel in the mouth with a shotgun.

Lionel was a former Buddhist monk who came to know the Lord through reading a tract that someone had thrown out of a car window. Following his conversion he felt called to the ministry and in time graduated from Bible college.

Lionel did not take the easy route and pastor a church in a Christian area of Sri Lanka, but instead went back to his home village of Tissamaharama where he faithfully served God for five years before he was brutally murdered.

Apart from the tract-throwing car driver, he was probably the first Christian worker to venture into this predominantly Buddhist area where there was certainly no Christian presence.

After his death, a cross was placed to mark his grave. It was the only cross to be found in this area covering 50 square miles, inhabited by nearly a million people. This cross was to become the symbol of the Living Christ, who changed the lives of many as Lalani, the widow of the martyr, returned from the funeral of her husband and vowed never to leave the place and cause for which her husband gave his life. His blood was to become the seed-plot of revival in the deep South of Sri Lanka.

Sister Lalani, as she is known, continued where

Lionel and Lalani Jayasinghe
Photo: Christian Solidarity Worldwide 2009

Lionel had left off. When the leaders of his church offered to move her to a safer location, she told them, 'Every time I see the blood stains of my husband splattered all over my house, each stain gives me courage to stay on and continue the vision for which he gave his life.'

She has been issued death threats; her church has been set on fire, destroying the roof; five bombs have been placed in the church (miraculously some of the bombs did not go off and those that did caused little damage; she has been surrounded by mobs and threatened; her home has been stoned continuously during one long night.

In spite of it all, Lalani stayed on, trusting in God. The area where she ministers in is an area very resistant to the gospel. Christian penetration was very low as this was a citadel of idol worship – a stronghold of Hindu and Buddhist deities, who are revered, feared and worshipped by millions. Even the British Colonial rulers did not penetrate this area during their 500 years of rule. But this courageous woman of God stays on, building on the foothold gained by her husband.

Lalani walks several miles a day in order to minister to the needy, sometimes spending the night in believers' homes as there is no public transportation. Signs and wonders accompany her powerful ministry.

She now has a congregation of 300 in the church she pastors, and there are now over 1,000 believers in the Tissamaharama area. She has established branch churches all over the Southern Province. These are the fruits of her faithful ministry among the people for whom Pastor Lionel gave his life.

The week before Lionel was killed, those who instigated his murder had said, 'We should have cut down this tree (his ministry) with our fingernails while it was small, now we have to use an axe.' Today, the mighty tree that God has nurtured through Lalani cannot be cut down by any axe … it has grown beyond the power of human effort or demonic influence.

As the Lord said: '… unless an ear of wheat falls to the ground and die, it remains alone; but if it dies, it produces much fruit' (John 12:24, NKJV). Lalani is a living proof of this.

WEEK FOUR
UNCOMFORTABLE
TRUTH

By Lyndon Bowring

AUTHOR PROFILE

Lyndon Bowring is Chairman of CARE, a UK charity which seeks to declare biblical truth and demonstrate Christ's compassion and address vital moral issues facing the nation. Lyndon was born in South Wales, studied at the London Bible College (now London School of Theology) and is an Elim minister, based at Kensington Temple. He is a member of the Evangelical Alliance Council and other Christian Boards and Councils of Reference. Lyndon is a well-known speaker at many Christian events and churches, and is also involved with several accountability groups of church leaders. Lyndon is married to Celia. They have three children in their early twenties.

INTRODUCTION

The testimony of Jeremiah in the following five days' notes is an awesome encouragement. He started his ministry at seventeen and finished well in later life. In the days ahead we meet characters we can relate to: a weak leader anxious to please men rather than God, a secret believer of high rank who comes to the prophet's rescue, and a ruthless, powerful king who tortures and imprisons those who defy him.

The story of how Jeremiah kept his faith and shared it courageously with others reminds us of our brothers and sisters undergoing severe persecution because they are loyal to the Lord Jesus. Let's pray they will hold fast to the promised hope; that one day every injustice will be righted and each believer saved by grace rewarded for what they have done and endured for His sake. Jeremiah – fully prepared to speak God's word with grace and suffer for his faithfulness – was remarkably vindicated, for everything he prophesied came to pass. Jeremiah willingly went into exile with the captives although he could have stayed at home. What's more, never once in his life did he say 'I told you so!' What a hero!

DAY 1

ZEDEKIAH'S WEAKNESS, JEREMIAH'S COURAGE

BIBLE READING
Jeremiah 37:1–17

KEY VERSE
'Then King Zedekiah sent for him and had him brought to the palace, where he asked him privately, "Is there any word from the LORD?" "Yes," Jeremiah replied, "you will be handed over to the king of Babylon."' (v.17)

Zedekiah was a weak king, flip-flopping between wanting to save his own skin and please his people, and worrying about the possibility of God's judgment. He summoned the prophet Jeremiah, who had been thrown into prison by the king's officials, and asked him to pray and prophesy in favour of the holy city of Jerusalem and its inhabitants. Like the rest of his court, Zedekiah could not believe that God would ever allow the enemy to overrun the City of David and destroy Solomon's magnificent Temple. Read 2 Chronicles 9:22–24 to glimpse the splendour and greatness of the world-famous Jerusalem, visited by all the monarchs on earth. As Jeremiah observed in Lamentations 4:12, 'The kings of the earth did not believe, nor did any of the world's peoples, that enemies and foes could enter the gates of Jerusalem.' It was as unthinkable an idea as it would be for us today to think of an invading foreign army marching on London and taking over Buckingham Palace and the Houses of Parliament.

Zedekiah wanted reassurance that God would come to the rescue but Jeremiah did not indulge him. Instead, he courageously delivered news that nobody wanted to hear. God would keep the promise to reward Israel's obedience with blessing and her disobedience with punishment (see Deut. 30:15–17). Time had run out for the Jews, and their repeated rejection of God over generations was about to reap a terrible harvest. The Babylonians were coming, to raze the city to the ground and capture the king and all his people. Jeremiah knew he must speak the truth even though it meant being accused of treason, facing suffering and death.

Zedekiah and the other leaders relied on past blessing and success to guarantee God's ongoing protection. This is an easy mistake to make; I know of several Christians with powerful ministries who believed that God would overlook their serious sin because of the obvious blessing on their lives. Let's always be vigilant and honour Him in both small and big things. May God help us to be true to our calling just as Jeremiah was – whatever the cost.

PRAYER

Almighty God, grant strength to Your servants who choose to stand for Your truth and speak out for justice whatever the cost to them. Amen.

DAY 2

IMPRISONED FOR HIS FAITH IN GOD

BIBLE READING
Jeremiah 37:18–38:7

KEY VERSE
'So they took Jeremiah and put him into the cistern of Malkijah, the king's son, which was in the courtyard of the guard. They lowered Jeremiah by ropes into the cistern; it had no water in it, only mud, and Jeremiah sank down into the mud.' (38:6)

Jeremiah's life was never easy. God appointed him to be a prophet from before he was born, and Jeremiah was probably about seventeen when he began prophesying. His family opposed him, and as he became involved in political matters and spoke out God's words, he came under further attack. But no matter what life threw at him, this faithful prophet was determined to obey the Lord and deliver His messages however hard that was.

Tens of thousands of our brothers and sisters today are persecuted because of their faith in Jesus. Some are shut away from the daylight, deprived of human company, badly treated and left there for years. Imagine the anguish of their families and friends, perhaps not knowing where they are and powerless to bring any relief. Place yourself in the position of the prisoners – 'Whatever will happen to me?' 'Is there no hope?' 'How can I stay sane and not give in to despair?' Thank God that He knows each one, and ask Him to show us how to reach out to these men and women effectively through our intercessions and by putting pressure on their captors.

Jeremiah was thrown into a dungeon, then given some respite and allowed to live in the prison courtyard and be fed. However, when his enemies learned that he had prophesied Jerusalem's downfall, they persuaded King Zedekiah to put him into Malkijah's cistern. This meant a slow death, drowning horribly in the four or five feet of soft mud at the bottom of this deep well whose narrow neck shut out most of the light.

Perhaps your life is a prison, although not literally behind bars you feel walled in by depression, an abusive relationship you cannot escape or the pain and suffering of illness or injury. In situations like these, it is difficult to find God – but He is nearer than you may think. Psalm 40:2 says, 'He lifted me out of the slimy pit, out of the mud and mire; he set my feet on a rock and gave me a firm place to stand'. Help is at hand, He is ready to hear us.

PRAYER

Heavenly Father, please be near people who are in prison today and give them comfort and hope. Stretch out Your hand to rescue and heal. Amen.

DAY 3

EBED-MELECH – BRAVE ADVOCATE

BIBLE READING
Jeremiah 38:7–10

KEY VERSE

'But Ebed-Melech, a Cushite, an official in the royal palace, heard that they had put Jeremiah into the cistern. While the king was sitting in the Benjamin Gate, Ebed-Melech went out of the palace and said to him, "My lord the king, these men have acted wickedly in all they have done to Jeremiah the prophet. They have thrown him into a cistern, where he will starve to death when there is no longer any bread in the city."' (vv.7–9)

Jeremiah's rescuer was an Ethiopian, presumably brought to Jerusalem as a slave and made a eunuch. 'Ebed-Melech' means 'servant of the king' – probably a title rather than his name – and it seems he held high rank. Ebed-Melech risked Zedekiah's anger to serve the King of kings, by pleading for Jeremiah.

God has His people in high

places. The Bible describes how Esther, the Jewish girl who married King Xerxes, was instrumental in saving her people from genocide. Writing to the Philippians, Paul spoke of the believers in Caesar's household. Many Christian believers today serve under oppressive regimes and must conceal their faith on pain of death. Pray for them to be protected, spiritually strengthened and able to be an influence for good in the midst of evil situations.

Brave and compassionate, Ebed-Melech was Jeremiah's true friend, not forgetting him in the midst of the turmoil of the besieged city. He dropped what he was doing and rushed to speak to the king and beg for mercy.

In our busy lives, may we remember to take time to speak up for those who have no voice. It is easy to leave it to someone else but maybe God is calling just ordinary people like you and me to be advocates for those who are hidden away and persecuted for their faith – and to pray for them too. We can easily find out more through organisations like Christian Solidarity Worldwide. This morning on the way to my office, I witnessed a peaceful procession of Chinese Malaysians and their supporters walking to the Home Office to ask for justice on behalf of these British Overseas Citizens who are denied the right to work and live here but cannot return to their own country. This coalition of concerned people included a number of Christians, and I was able to pray with them.

Jesus' parable of the Good Samaritan demonstrates that it is often the stranger in our communities who shows most compassion. May we be ready to respond to any prompting God gives us to reach out to those in other parts of the world who need our support.

PRAYER

Thank You, Lord, for people like Ebed-Melech, who are willing to identify with those in prison and work for their release. Please raise up more Christians to do the same today. Amen.

DAY 4

THE COMPASSION OF EBED-MELECH

BIBLE READING
Jeremiah 38:11–13

KEY VERSE
'He took some old rags and worn-out clothes from there and let them down with ropes to Jeremiah in the cistern. Ebed-Melech the Cushite said to Jeremiah, "Put these old rags and worn-out clothes under your arms to pad the ropes."' (vv.11–12)

By the time Ebed-Melech had got together the thirty men the king had assigned to the task of saving the prophet and arrived back at the cistern, Jeremiah must have been desperate, eking out the last ounces of his strength to keep from slipping into the suffocating ooze at the bottom of the dark pit. Realising how weak he would be, Ebed-Melech not only threw Jeremiah a lifeline, but also lowered a

Pastor Simon is a theologian, Baptist minister and refugee. From his Bible college in Mae La refugee camp, he seeks to serve the displaced Karen people of Burma.

Joel Cruz Garcia was killed for refusing to renounce his faith. His widow Yuvy continues to spread the Word in unsettled Columbia.

Father Calciu was imprisoned for preaching the gospel in Nicolae Ceauşescu's highly repressive Romania. But being held captive could not stop the good news, as he led his cellmates to Christ.

Carlos Lamelas called for religious freedom in Cuba. He was arrested by the government on false charges, but he and his family can bear witness to God's wonderful faithfulness.

Pastor George Orji held fast to his faith right up to the moment of his brutal murder at the hands of Nigeria's militant Islamist group Boko Haram.

Sister Lourdes and the institute she founded share the love of Christ in practical ways with the poor and needy of East Timor.

The murder of Pastor Lionel Jayasinghe could not stop revival in Sri Lanka. Lionel's wife Lalani is ministering to the needy and planting new churches in a predominantly Buddhist area.

Well-known Eritrean gospel singer Helen Berhane has suffered severe torture because of her faith.

bundle of rags to make the rope less painful under the armpits. Little by little they lifted him out into the safety of the courtyard.

This story reminds us of God's love. He not only delivers us from danger but also provides over and above what is necessary. There's an old hymn about how Jesus rescues us from the power of sin and death. He was willing to give His life on the cross, to give us eternal life:

I was sinking deep in sin, sinking to rise no more
Overwhelmed by sin within, mercy I did implore
Then the Master of the sea heard my imploring cry
Christ my Saviour lifted me, now saved am I!

Love lifted me! Love lifted me!
When no one but Christ could help, Love lifted me.
James Rowe (1865–1933)

We may not be involved in a rescue mission as dramatic as Ebed-Melech's, but opportunities to offer practical care to people in need will still arise. The gift of hospitality involves sharing what we have with others – whether that is a welcome into our actual home or through financial and other practical support. Christians facing persecution frequently need this kind of help. The Good Samaritan picked up the wounded traveller, tended his wounds and then arranged with a nearby inn to care for him, not expecting any recompense for his actions. At times we all need the comfort of a friend, the gentleness of someone who cares, the reassurance that we are safe when we are assailed with fears and doubts. Like Ebed-Melech and the Good Samaritan, we can be the hands and feet of Jesus Himself.

PRAYER

Heavenly Father, please fill us with Your compassion for those in need and guide us in our giving – whatever form that may take. Amen.

GOD OF JUSTICE AND MERCY

BIBLE READING
Jeremiah 39:1–18

KEY VERSE
'... This is what the LORD Almighty, the God of Israel, says: I am about to fulfil my words against this city through disaster, not prosperity. At that time they will be fulfilled before your eyes. But I will rescue you on that day, declares the LORD; you will not be handed over to those you fear.'
(vv.16–17)

After two and a half years of siege and starvation, Jerusalem finally fell and Nebuchadnezzar, king of Babylon, victoriously marched in and took over. As Jeremiah had prophesied, Zedekiah's life was spared but he was forced to witness the killing of his sons, was then blinded and taken off to Babylon in chains. Jeremiah was set free and vindicated as the truthful prophet.

We worship a God of perfect

justice – but His nature is also to show mercy. However, looking around our troubled world and the undeserved suffering of so many of those whom He loves, we may sometimes wonder why such wicked people, corrupt regimes and evil ideologies dominate so much. We may even be tempted to doubt God's love and integrity. But, as the apostle Paul wrote, a day of fearful judgment is coming when all these wrongs will be righted:

> ... [God's] righteous judgment will be revealed. God
> 'will give to each person according to what he has
> done'. To those who by persistence in doing good seek
> glory, honour and immortality, he will give eternal life.
> But for those who are self-seeking and who reject the
> truth and follow evil, there will be wrath and anger.
>
> Romans 2:5–8

When we finally reach heaven, I believe that we will see millions of men, women and children who suffered terribly in this life in seats of great honour and receiving riches untold from the King they loved and served to the point of death. We should tremble at the thought of God's righteous anger towards those who rejected His ways and regularly examine our own lives and confess our sins. But often punishments and rewards come to us during our lifetimes. Just as Zedekiah met his brutal fate, so Ebed-Melech received a special message of mercy and grace from God. His courage, compassion and commitment to his friend Jeremiah did not go unnoticed. The same is true of our actions and expressions of loyalty to God's people. We can trust the Judge of all the earth to do right (see Gen. 18:25).

PRAYER

Holy God, we long for Christ's coming when all wrongs will be put right and Your faithful servants will be rewarded. We place our trust in Your righteousness, forgiveness, mercy and grace. Amen.

THE STORY OF
PASTOR SIMON

Situated on the border of Thailand and Burma is Mae La
refugee camp. Home to well over 30,000 refugees, it is the
largest of nine such camps, providing sanctuary to people
fleeing the brutal military regime that terrorises Burma.
The refugees are predominantly from the Karen ethnic
group which straddles Burma's eastern border.

      The Karen people, along with the Karenni, Shan and
other ethnic nationalities in Burma, have been struggling
for freedom ever since Burma's independence at the end of
the Second World War. Perhaps forty per cent of Karens are
Christian, mainly Baptist.

      These people have fled one of the worst regimes
in the world. Burma is ruled by a military junta
which seized power in a coup in 1962, held elections
in 1990, overwhelmingly lost those elections to the
democracy leader Aung San Suu Kyi, but rejected the
results, imprisoned the victors and intensified its grip
on power. In Karen State and the other ethnic areas, the
military is carrying out a campaign of ethnic cleansing
and, arguably, attempted genocide. Forced labour, the
forcible conscription of child soldiers, the use of human
minesweepers, torture, rape and killing are widespread and
systematic. More than a million people have been driven
from their homes into the jungle, hundreds of thousands
have fled the country, and since 1996 over 3,300 villages in
eastern Burma have been destroyed. It is a regime guilty of
virtually every possible human rights violation, amounting
to crimes against humanity.

      On the edge of Mae La camp sits a Bible college,

housed in a fragile, simple bamboo structure, with the words of Psalm 33:12 over the entrance: 'Blessed is the nation whose God is the LORD, the people whom He has chosen as his heritage.' Underneath is Psalm 34:14: 'Turn from evil and do good; seek peace and pursue it.' The college is led by the Reverend Doctor Simon, sometimes known as Pastor Simon, a theologian, Baptist minister and refugee.

Pastor Simon has made a conscious choice in life: to serve his people. A lecturer at a seminary in Rangoon, specialising in biblical theology, particularly the Old Testament, he fled to the border following the regime's brutal crackdown on pro-democracy protests in 1988, in which at least 3,000 died. He could easily have gone

Pastor Simon
Photo: Christian Solidarity Worldwide 2009

abroad, not as a refugee, but as an academic. Indeed, he had previously pursued his doctoral work in the Philippines for two years, and had returned to Rangoon just a year before the crackdown. During the protests, he organised public prayer gatherings and provided pastoral care for the demonstrating students. He fled, along with others, when his own life was in danger. 'We could hear shooting all night,' he recalled. 'There were rumours that the water and food had been poisoned. There was no security. Life was very insecure.'

To disguise their escape, Pastor Simon and his wife made a number of preliminary journeys out of Rangoon, into Karen State, for Bible study sessions, so that when they finally left for good, the authorities assumed they were just on another church outing. They endured a hazardous two-month journey through the jungle, across mountains and rivers, carrying whatever they could on their backs, accompanied by thirteen others. Pastor Simon's elderly father-in-law had to be carried the whole way.

Upon reaching Thailand, it would not have been impossible with his academic credentials, for Pastor Simon to make his way to the West. But he knew God's call on his life was to stay with his fellow refugees. He was invited to teach at a Karen Bible school in a place called Wallay, and soon became Principal of the Kawthoolei Karen Bible School and College. A year after he arrived, Wallay was attacked by the Burma Army, and Pastor Simon and his students moved to Mae La camp, where he re-established the school. In 1990, he had four or five teachers and forty-five students.

In the past twenty years, Pastor Simon's Bible school has gained international recognition. Teachers from the Philippines, Korea, India, Australia, the United States and elsewhere come each year, and hundreds of students have graduated. The Baptist World Alliance and the Asian

Baptist Federation have accredited the school, and in 1993
a Bachelor of Theology programme was added to the
curriculum. Three years later, a Bachelor of Arts degree
was offered, providing courses in political science, history,
economics, education and English.

In 2000, the Baptist World Alliance recognised
with their Human Rights Award Pastor Simon's remarkable
work. The previous recipient was former US President
Jimmy Carter. But Pastor Simon was unable to travel to
receive the award. The Thai authorities told him that if he
could find a sponsor, he could leave Thailand – but could
not return. 'I am here to help and live with my people,' he
said. 'If I went and could not come back, I could not help
my people – so I did not go.'

Pastor Simon was born on 19 July 1949 – known
as Martyrs Day in Burma, and the day when the Karen
struggle for freedom began. In his teens, he made a personal
commitment to Christ but, he says now, his faith was
nominal and he lacked 'a deep understanding of salvation'.
In 1965 he had a series of dreams, which changed the
course of his life.

'I dreamed that I was flying over mountains, rivers
and seas, and I had a peculiar kind of peace,' he recalls.
'After these dreams I just knew that God was about to do
something to change my life.'

A bright student and keen athlete, he competed in
marathons. On one occasion, he spent two entire days
running, competing in a 5,000-metre race, a 10,000-metre
race and a marathon. At the end he collapsed, exhausted
and unable to breathe. 'I thought I was dying. I prayed for
God's healing power. I told Him that if He healed me, I
would do whatever he wanted. The doctor checked me and
concluded that the only thing wrong was over-exercise, and
told me to drink lots of water and rest for a month.' While
recuperating, a nurse told him of her desire to help people

study in Bible school, and asked him if he was interested.
He felt a door had opened.

English is not Pastor Simon's first language, it is
probably his fourth or fifth. He speaks Karen, Burmese
and Thai too. Yet his English is extraordinary, and he
composes prayers and meditations in English from his
simple bamboo home in the refugee camp. One such
meditation reflects both his spirit, his intellect and his
simplicity, and speaks of the faith of the persecuted
and displaced:

I am not ashamed to be a refugee, for I know my Lord, my
    Master, my Saviour,
Was a refugee long, long before me.
I am not afraid to be a refugee, for though I am displaced,
    I am not misplaced.
I will never feel lonely, for God gives me many friends
    around the world.
I will never feel helpless, for God gives me many hands for help.
I will never stop doing good things in spite of all the
    difficulties and hardships, for I know that this is the
    real purpose of life God has entrusted to each one of us.
I will never feel regret being a refugee, for though life is
    full of limitations, restrictions and tragedies, it is
    enriched with meanings and values.
I will never feel hopeless, for my Saviour has promised me
    an eternal home.
I am glad to be a refugee for I am always reminded that
    my eternal home is in heaven and not on this earth.
But I know that for the time being, Satan is trying to
    enslave me, for though I live in my Father's, my
    brothers' and sisters' world, I am not free to travel.
However I am strongly convinced that a day will come
    – and it will be soon – that I will be able to travel
    freely to visit my brothers and sisters around the world

and say 'Thank you' for what they have done.
I will see the beauty of my Father's world. Amen.

Speaking of the crisis in Burma and his life as a refugee,
Pastor Simon has this message of hope:

> We want to go home. We want peace to be restored
> to our country so that we can go back. But though
> things around seem very dark and dim, we are strongly
> convinced that the Lord is in control of all and He will
> intervene and change the situation in Burma … It is His
> word that keeps us focusing our eyes on the Lord Jesus
> Christ and gives us hope to struggle and try the best we
> can to serve Him through serving His sons and daughters.
> Please pray, work hard and be prepared to help when the
> time comes for our repatriation. Our God is able, and He
> will intervene and reveal His mighty power for His glory
> and honour.

WEEK FIVE
IN THE WORLD
BUT NOT
OF THE WORLD

By Martin Smyth

AUTHOR PROFILE

W. Martin Smyth is a graduate in Arts and Divinity. He is an ordained minister in the Presbyterian Church of Ireland. He was ordained in Raffrey, County Down and pastored Alexandra Church, Belfast from 1963 to 1982.

After the murder of Robert Bradford MP, Martin represented Belfast South in Westminster from 1982 to 2005.

Martin is married to Kathleen, and they have two daughters and four grandchildren. Their third daughter was killed in a traffic accident.

INTRODUCTION

I was aware of problems facing Christians in the New Testament era, but the witness of Richard Wurmbrand awakened me to modern persecution. My congregation, though Presbyterian, was ready to provide refuge for the Siberian Seven Pentecostals, which they subsequently received in the United States.

Elected to Parliament, I learnt of the plight of Soviet Refusniks. These Jews were not only prevented from leaving Russia, but were also denied work in their professions and had to undertake menial labour and suffer other restrictions. I therefore joined the team which campaigned for their freedom and in Moscow saw their plight.

Alerted by the Jubilee Trust to persecution of Christians in Burma, and aware of the jihad massacre in the Molucca Islands of Indonesia, I initiated an adjournment debate in the first Parliament to focus on the issue. Later, with a CSW team and other parliamentarians, I experienced some of the people's suffering, and highlighted it to President, parliament and police.

First-hand experience in Sudan, Peru and Columbia gave me a deeper understanding of 'bearing the cross' and of challenging governments that subscribe to the UN declaration but do not allow the basic right of freedom to chose one's faith. Thus in caring for my brethren, I am doing it for Christ.

WEEK FIVE

DAY 1

IN THE WORLD BUT NOT OF THE WORLD

BIBLE READING
Daniel 1:1–5

KEY VERSE
'Then the king ordered Ashpenaz, chief of his court officials, to bring in some of the Israelites ... to serve in the king's palace.' (vv.3–4)

Christians are first and foremost citizens of heaven. But when the Lord Jesus prayed in John 17 for His disciples and those who would believe in Him through their message, He pleaded not that they be taken out of the world, but that they would be protected from the evil one.

Like Daniel and his friends, we live in a hostile environment. While religious liberty is prized by most in the UK, already signs are evident of growing intolerance in an increasingly secularised society. We may not be faced with the sort of antagonism that Daniel and the Israelites experienced or know the vicious animosity that Jesus and His Church experience in other nations – nevertheless, a challenge faces us as believers. And when things happen contrary to our expectations and understanding, we regularly utter that most human cry, 'Why, Lord?' But then we remember that God's ways are not always our ways – as we see in the stories of the sufferings of Job; of the disciple James executed early in his service; and of the aged John suffering in exile on Patmos (Job; Rev. 1:9; and Acts 12:2).

One of the tragedies of the last century and this one is the way in which the world has dithered while thousands have been murdered and millions displaced in the Sudan. I remember a scene near Juba, where I was privileged to speak with a young pastor who was deputising for a wounded colleague. This colleague was being treated in Uganda as he had been one of a number of Christians who had boldly put a cross on top of his hut so that bombers acting on the orders of the National Islamic Front would target him rather than his non-Christian neighbours. We are called not simply to a conversion experience with a reservation in heaven but to a life of discipleship. We must take up our cross and follow Christ (Mark 8:34). Those of us living in more secure and settled societies would do well to remember our brothers and sisters in Christ who face greater hostility, and uphold them in prayer and, where possible, practically and in advocacy.

PRAYER
Our Father and Sovereign Lord, we thank You for Your mercy and grace in Christ Jesus, and plead that we and our brothers and sisters elsewhere be kept faithful. Amen.

# WEEK FIVE

DAY 2

TEMPTED AND TESTED

BIBLE READING
Daniel 1:6–8

KEY VERSE
'But Daniel resolved not to defile himself with the royal food and wine, and he asked the chief official for permission not to defile himself in this way.' (v.8)

Most of us love good food and would gladly eat a royal feast. The rest of us may be more selective and only pick at our food. This was a problem for Peter in Acts 10. He had a vision of a large sheet descending from heaven, containing all kinds of animals, reptiles and birds. The instruction that came with it was: 'Kill and eat' (v.13). His response, 'Surely not, Lord!', brought the rebuke not to 'call anything impure that God has made clean'. This response has been used by some Christians to excuse questionable choices. They ignore the later guidance from the Jerusalem Council in Acts 15 and Paul's reminder of our responsibility to weaker brethren (see 1 Cor. 8:9).

Like Daniel and his friends, sooner or later we have choices to make which often impinge on our loyalty to the Lord Jesus or self-interest. As captives of Nebuchadnezzar, the offer of privileges in the service of the king must have been very attractive to young men facing an insecure future. Food and drink from the palace, a good education in Babylon's language and literature and a bright future in the service of the king. In this age of a prosperity gospel, the preferred option of a materialistic lifestyle would be a subtle attraction. But Daniel, Hananiah, Mishael and Azariah were of sterner stuff. They chose not to defile themselves by accepting the offer, and asked the chief official to excuse them.

Similar temptations still test us, whether in totalitarian states or liberal democracies. Christians are pressurised to conform to prevailing mores or obey legislation which demands loyalty to a state rather than to Jesus Christ. The choice is clear. We are to be transformers for a new society and not conformers to anything which denies Jesus' lordship. Such a choice has meant martyrdom at the hands of fanatics or the sanction of states. It has entailed imprisonment, torture and expulsion from family or community. Recently in the United Kingdom, it has cost people their jobs and livelihoods and has led to court cases.

May we be found faithful to our Lord and uphold those facing temporal consequences for their loyalty to their Lord and Saviour.

PRAYER
Grant, loving Father, discernment to all Your children, that we may know to chose right and eschew wrong when faced with subtle temptations. Amen.

WEEK FIVE

DAY 3

FRIENDS IN STRANGE PLACES

BIBLE READING
Daniel 1:9–10

KEY VERSE
'Now God caused the official to show favour and sympathy to Daniel …'
(v.9)

With **modern scientific** mindsets, it is easy to forget that we serve an Almighty God who is not confined by territorial boundaries or ecclesiastical buildings. Even in places where His existence is denied, there are humans made in His likeness and endowed with 'common grace', ready to risk their lives to help others. The chief of Nebuchadnezzar's household was one such person. Although under the authority of a king who would not hesitate to execute him if he failed in his duties, he showed sympathy to Daniel. And God honoured not only Daniel and his friends' faith but also the official's care of his charges.

God still has His way in strange places. As He used the commander of the guard in Jerusalem to provide an escort to protect Paul (Acts 23:12–35), so today there are instances where help is given to Christians in prison. Sometimes it might be food or encouragement. On other occasions it has enabled believers to escape from places like Vietnam. Such provision is not only miraculous but also marvellous in our eyes, and we can praise God for it.

However, a word of caution as we pray for persecuted brothers and sisters. Regularly we tend to pray that God would deliver them from such trials. The Lord Jesus was tried, but He submitted to the Father's will (Luke 22:39–46). We should also pray that believers stand strong in their faith, knowing that God uses trials to purify and strengthen His Church.

There is also the challenge for those of us who may not face fines, imprisonment, exile or death because of our faith in the Lord Jesus. Do we really care for those parts of His Body, the Church, suffering for His sake? As we thank God for His deliverances, we need to remember that 'faith without deeds is dead' (James 2:26). The challenge, therefore, is: What are we doing to help our persecuted brothers and sisters? Are we engaged in the work of prayer for them? Is there a place in our tithing for gifts either directly or through agencies supporting them? In our internet society, have we lost the art of writing a note of support to a lonely prisoner?

PRAYER
Thank You, Father God, for raising helpers in strange places. Please stir our hearts, that we may be motivated to act in support of those suffering for Christ. Amen.

WEEK FIVE

DAY 4

FAITH RECOMPENSED

BIBLE READING
Daniel 1:11–17

KEY VERSE
'At the end of the ten days they looked healthier and better nourished than any of the young men who ate the royal food.' (v.15)

Christians, like Gideon of old (Judges 6:17ff), have often sought signs from God that they are doing the right thing. In this passage, a captive pleads with his guard to test him and his friends before demanding them to act against their creed and conscience. Daniel does it with no degree of arrogance; rather, his request is courteous: 'Please test your servants ...' (v.12).

Daniel wanted the guard to see

that his God was able to keep His people. Daniel's faith was being tried. Did God care? Would He provide? Consent was given. Instead of the rich food the king provided, Daniel and his friends had a vegetarian diet, with water to drink, for ten days. And the four young men came through the ten days successfully.

John Noble, in his book *I found God in Soviet Russia*,* recorded a remarkable incident which showed God is still in control when His children are imprisoned for their faith. A woman prisoner was refused food because she would not deny her faith in the Lord Jesus. To the amazement of her tormentors, she did not fade away but rather flourished. They sought to find who was nourishing her with sustenance. But there was no evidence of any human or earthly provider. God fed her without even using ravens as he had for Elijah (see 1 Kings 17:6).

More recently, in Indonesia there was the case of a woman pastor sentenced for teaching children about Jesus the friend of children. She continued to minister to her congregation as they visited her in the prison, so the message of Christ was spread to guards and other prisoners.

Thankfully, God still cares for His children in captivity or facing other forms of persecution. As in Daniel's case, He may use in the process a kindly-disposed guard. On other occasions, He will use the prayers of people like us.

PRAYER
Thank You, Jesus, for sharing with us in our afflictions. May prison guards and persecutors learn, as did Saul of Tarsus, that You are the One they persecute, and go on to discover the joy of Your forgiveness. Amen.

*John Noble, *I found God in Soviet Russia* (Grand Rapids: Zondervan, 1972).

DAY 5

GOD VINDICATES HIS CHILDREN

BIBLE READING
Daniel 1:18–21

KEY VERSE
'The king talked with them, and he found none equal to Daniel, Hananiah, Mishael and Azariah; so they entered the king's service.' (v.19)

While the world may deride, scorn or persecute Christians, God still vindicates them. So it was with Daniel and his companions. When the trial ended, their appearance and physique were clearly superior to those who had fared sumptuously on the royal food and wine. Therefore, the guard took away the choice food and served them their chosen vegetables and water. He may even have made some profit for himself from their abstemiousness.

Christians continue to be persecuted. This may be by government decree, mob violence, communists or fanatics of other religions, or it may be for personal gain. Nevertheless, God knows those who are His, and He never forsakes them. Like Job, these Christians may not fully understand what is happening to them, but they can confidently maintain their belief in their loving Saviour who will deliver them.

Visiting Indonesia with a parliamentary delegation of Christian and Muslim members, accompanied by a Christian Solidarity Worldwide staffer, I was thrilled to hear Christian students, who knew what persecution meant, lovingly declare their faith in the Lord Jesus and their willingness to suffer for Him. This was at a time when a Christian pastor and some young people were paying dearly for their service, and even moderate Muslims living at peace with Christian neighbours suffered at the hands of Islamic jihadists.

What a challenge for those of us living in the comparative freedom of the UK, a nominal Christian society, to be faithful to our faithful Lord and to support our suffering sisters and brothers. God uses people today as He used Daniel's keeper. This may include personal involvement or financial support – even in the Credit Crunch – for agencies working with and for persecuted Christians. It certainly will mean prayerful remembrance as we uphold them at the throne of grace. There is also the challenge to care for the stranger of another colour, class or creed to us, who is suffering because of intolerant people in our society. It could also involve us in campaigning against legislation, albeit in the guise of equality, that is being used to undermine Christian standards.

PRAYER

Righteous Lord, we praise You that redeemed by Your blood we are clothed in Your righteousness. We thank You that You vindicate Your children. So, we commit to Your care and deliverance our persecuted brothers and sisters. Amen.

THE STORY OF
HELEN BERHANE

'The helicopter' is a notoriously painful torture position
where one's legs and arms are bound together for lengthy
periods of time ...

A well-known gospel singer from Eritrea called
Helen Berhane has not only experienced and withstood
'the helicopter', but has been locked in a poorly ventilated
metal shipping container for months and received crippling
beatings for being a committed Christian.

Would you go through it?

Helen's popular CD of songs about Jesus and her bold
evangelism made her a target for the Eritrean authorities. As
a member of Rhema Pentecostal Church, one of over thirty
churches that effectively became illegal in Eritrea in May
2002, Helen walked a fine and dangerous line by continuing
to evangelise and write successful gospel music. She knew
what her fearlessness might lead to. After the Eritrean
government ordered the closure of every church except those
belonging to the Catholic, Orthodox and Evangelical Lutheran
denominations, Helen knew it was only a matter of time before
she was identified as being part of a banned church. Her skill
as a singer-songwriter had become widely known in Eritrea.

She was arrested in May 2004, incarcerated in Mai
Serwa army camp and tortured so horrifically that each
dawn brought with it an intense feeling of dread.

> Even though I walk through the valley of the shadow of
> death, I will fear no evil, for you are with me; your rod
> and your staff, they comfort me.
>
> Psalm 23:4

The use of torture is routine in Eritrean detention centres and all detainees experience severe mistreatment at the hands of the government. Despite this, Helen, who was also mother to an eleven-year-old, refused to renounce her Christian faith.

When human rights groups began to pressure the Eritrean government for Helen's release, the authorities initially responded by inflicting yet more pain on her. During the last and most appalling assault, Helen was taken aside by a guard and beaten almost to death, receiving no medical attention until several months later.

'I was beaten from head to toe, and especially on the legs and abdomen. This caused damage to my liver and kidneys. Later, when the doctors examined me, they could

Helen Berhane
Photo: Christian Solidarity Worldwide 2009

see the damage, but were amazed to find that the liver and kidneys had somehow healed themselves. Even they saw this as miraculous.'

Helen used to be a keen sportswoman, but was left disabled by this final assault. When news of the beating became known, the international spotlight eventually led to her being placed under house arrest in October 2006.

Despite being severely disabled, the singer managed to escape to Sudan with her sister. Her daughter Eva was later smuggled across the border from Eritrea with the help of nomads. Unaware that she was now Eritrea's most well-known detainee, Helen thought she was safe, but the Eritrean authorities were still looking for her. They regularly raid Sudan to recover refugees and force them to return.

During their ten-month exile in Sudan, Helen and Eva couldn't settle. They moved house on several occasions and desperately prayed for a way to find safety. Christian Solidarity Worldwide (CSW), the international human rights charity, lobbied the British government in an attempt to secure them citizenship in the UK, but eventually, Denmark granted them sanctuary.

Today, Helen can barely walk and going out without a wheelchair is almost impossible for her. Panic attacks continue, but her faith remains strong and she is determined to do whatever she can to highlight the suffering of Eritrean Christians who are still languishing in detention centres on account of their faith.

In an interview with CSW Helen thanked people who prayed for her: 'There is a saying in my native Tigrinya that loosely translates: a person can only value you to the degree of their own value. I have been blessed and honoured by your love and that says a lot about your value as brothers and sisters.'

There are few men or women with the courage

Helen possesses, but would Helen have written Christian songs and released an album if she knew what torture she would have to face? Her lyrics say she still would have.

Although Helen Berhane now lives in a safe house in Denmark, there are still close to 3,000 Christians detained in Eritrea, many of whom are being tortured every day.

WEEK SIX
THE RETURN
OF THE KING

By David Coffey

AUTHOR PROFILE

David Coffey OBE is the President of the Baptist World Alliance and Global Ambassador for BMS World Mission.

David has visited eighty countries in all the continents, but he has a particular interest in the Middle East and seeks to strengthen the work and witness of the churches of the Arab world. His human rights visits include China, Egypt, Cuba, Russia, Azerbaijan and Vietnam.

David has been married to his wife Janet for forty-four years, and they have two adult children and four grandchildren. His interests are soccer, music and political biography.

INTRODUCTION

Imagine if the government of your country did one or more of the following things:

- banned all worship services in church buildings
- demanded that symbols of the cross were removed
- permitted Christians to hold meetings but made singing hymns illegal
- outlawed any translations of the Bible.

Many Christians do not have to imagine this scenario; it is their living experience. Their story is one of inspiring courage and faith and it brings alive the verse from the book of Revelation 'They overcame him by the blood of the Lamb and by the word of their testimony; they did not love their lives so much as to shrink from death' (Rev. 12:11).

Meeting the believers of the Persecuted Church sends you back to Scripture to discover sources of wisdom and comfort. This week we are considering the words of Jesus in Matthew 25 and the theme of judgment. Christians who are forbidden to practise their faith can draw comfort from God's ultimate justice. Those who are intercessors need this 'end times' perspective of Jesus. God the King *will* have the last word on human history and every human being *will* be held accountable to Him.

WEEK SIX

DAY 1

JESUS THE KING IS COMING

BIBLE READING
Matthew 25:31–46

KEY VERSE
'When the Son of Man comes in his glory, and all the angels with him, he will sit on his throne in heavenly glory.' (v.31)

We live in turbulent times when believers face constant danger to their lives. In such times the Word of God says we are to prepare for the return of King Jesus. Each day this week, I would ask you to meditate on our Bible reading, Matthew 25:31–46, and each day I will focus on a particular verse from that passage. When the disciples asked Jesus 'what will be the sign of your coming and of the end of the age?'

(Matt. 24:3), He predicted there would be: turbulent times when reliable landmarks would disappear (vv.1–2); religious confusion when false prophets would lead people astray (vv.4–5); and dangerous days of suffering for believers, the like of which had not been seen since the beginning of time (v.21).

Jesus encouraged His disciples in the midst of turbulence, confusion and danger to 'keep watch' for His coming in glory. In this long section of teaching (Matt. 23–25) Jesus provides four brilliant picture parables which reveal how we can prepare for His coming.

The picture of the burglar teaches us to be vigilant (Matt. 24:42–44). Just as the burglar comes without warning, so the coming of the Lord will be like 'a thief in the night' (1 Thess. 5:2).

The picture of the butler teaches us to be reliable (Matt. 24:45–51). The diligent servant cares for the needs of the household and even when the master is not physically at home, he serves as if the master is present.

The picture of the bridesmaids teaches us to be faithful (Matt. 25:1–13). Keeping a ready supply of oil in order to shine your light for Jesus is a powerful symbol for Christian witness (Matt. 5:16).

The picture of the talents teaches us to be creative with God's investment (Matt. 25:14–30). The Lord has invested in our lives, abilities and opportunities, and we must use them responsibly until He returns. The quantity of the investment will vary; the issue is how we use what God has invested in our lives.

Jesus the King will return in glory, meanwhile:

- be vigilant as you wait
- be reliable as you serve
- be faithful as you witness
- be imaginative as you work.

PRAYER

Lord, keep me faithful as I wait for Your coming in glory. Give me power to be active in Your service. Through Jesus Christ our Lord. Amen.

JESUS THE JUDGE IS HERE

BIBLE READING
Matthew 25:31–46

KEY VERSE
'All the nations will be gathered before Him, and he will separate the people one from another as a shepherd separates the sheep from the goats.' (v.32)

I have just received an email detailing the latest outbreak of atrocious persecutions against the Christian community in Pakistan. It is heartbreaking news and all within me cries out for justice for the oppressed. Justice is one of the most powerful instincts of the human heart, and prompts believers to sing, 'Restore, O Lord, the honour of your name.'

The pledge of Jesus is that one

day He will come as the Judge, and His judgment will be based on how people have treated the members of His family. Jesus says the poor and needy of these verses are His family (Matt. 25:40) and He defines His brothers and sisters as those who do the will of His Father in heaven (Matt. 12:50).

The pastoral scene of sheep and goats as an illustration of judgment would have been meaningful to those listening to the teaching of Jesus. During the daytime it was not easy to distinguish similarly coloured sheep and goats, but at evening the shepherd could make a clear distinction, as the less hardy goats would head to a sheltered place for warmth. Sheep directed to the right and goats to the left was the ancient way of symbolising judgment for good and bad deeds.

Jesus makes it plain that when the King comes there will be a final judgment. Although people may appear indistinguishable, the judgment of Jesus will reveal those who have been true servants and served the poor and needy, and those who have only paid lip service to Jesus.

If a shepherd can make an accurate judgment to separate sheep and goats, we can trust Jesus the Judge to discern how His brothers and sisters have been treated (Matt. 25:40,45). Remember, the judgment of Jesus hinges on how we respond to His family when they are in need and the reference to 'All the nations ... gathered before him' indicates that no one escapes this moment of judgment.

PRAYER

Lord, I remember those who face injustice and persecution, and pray that their faith will not fail. Draw close to those who are suffering and grant them Your peace. Amen.

KEEP ON KEEPING ON

BIBLE READING
Matthew 25:31–46

KEY VERSE
'Then the King will say to those on his right, "Come, you who are blessed by my Father; take your inheritance, the kingdom prepared for you since the creation of the world."' (v.34)

DAY 3

'Compassion fatigue' is a challenge to those who make a commitment to be a voice for the voiceless. I have a friend who works in Africa, and his ministry brings him face to face with the daily violence and oppression faced by Christians there. His organisation is a stunning example of the 'keep on keeping on' principle of mercy ministries, which brings comfort and hope to thousands of oppressed people.

He shared with me how one day he stared out of his office window at the faces of the hundreds of hungry and homeless people who were queuing to be fed and housed, and he said to the Lord, 'I can't go on serving You here anymore.' The ministry of caring had overwhelmed him and he was about to quit. Then he heard the Lord saying, 'I am not asking you to do everything to change the world – this is not your task. Simply see Me in the faces of the poor and I will give you the strength to serve.' He stayed to minister.

The maths of these verses (Matt. 25:31–46) are overwhelming when they are broken down and studied carefully. Six human needs are mentioned four times: hunger; thirst; being a stranger; nakedness; sickness; and imprisonment. On three occasions the list of needs is accompanied by a list of remedies: something to eat; something to drink; an invitation to hospitality; the gift of clothing; the ministry of caring; and the ministry of visitation.

On the face of it, the challenge is overwhelming, but Jesus never said it would be easy to serve Him in these areas of need. He asks us to see His face in the faces of the poor and marginalised (vv.35–36). This is a costly ministry and it will bring us close to despair at times, but Jesus says it carries a spiritual reward which has been prepared from eternity. This is solid assurance for believers ministering in a hostile world.

PRAYER

Lord, give me the spiritual stamina to go on serving You today. Help me to see You in the faces of those to whom I minister. Amen.

WEEK SIX / DAY 4

SERVING OTHERS MEANS SERVING JESUS

BIBLE READING
Matthew 25:31–46

KEY VERSE
'The King will reply, "I tell you the truth, whatever you did for one of the least of these brothers of mine, you did for me."' (v.40)

There is an amazing principle at the heart of this verse which is underlined by the words of Jesus, 'I tell you the truth'. Whenever this phrase occurs in the Gospels, it is a statement of vital importance and not to be missed!

The amazing truth is that when we serve the needs of any family member of Jesus, however insignificant ('one of the least', v.40), we are serving Jesus Himself. This close, intimate relationship between Jesus and His disciples is found in other parts of the New Testament (1 Cor. 8.12; 12:27).

This truth is an encouragement to those of us who are part of the family of God, but it is a solemn warning to those who persecute the Body of Christ. The root meaning of the word 'persecute' is 'to pursue a prey'. Jesus knew that those who identified with Him would be hunted down by those who hated righteousness in order to be reviled and slandered. Those who reject Christ hate those who have chosen to love and follow the Saviour of the World, and they cannot see that in their hatred of believers they are persecuting Jesus (Acts 9:5).

In many parts of the world today there is fierce opposition to any form of Christian witness and presence. Teaching the Bible to children is forbidden; permission to open churches is refused; it is illegal to change your faith. Many believers are tortured and killed in terrifying circumstances.

The courageous witness of the Persecuted Church is an example of how to resist the devil and stand firm in the faith (1 Pet. 5:8–9). The persecuted use all the resources that God provides. They pray. They use the Word of God. They receive encouragement from other believers. They rebuke the enemy. Above all, they know that when they are persecuted, their wounds are a sign that they have been counted worthy to suffer for His name. And Jesus is intimately present with them in their pain.

PRAYER
Lord, help me to be a voice for the voiceless and to speak for those who cannot speak for themselves. Please strengthen those who are under attack for their faith. Amen.

TWO DESTINIES

BIBLE READING
Matthew 25:31–46

KEY VERSE
'Then they will go away to eternal punishment, but the righteous to eternal life.' (v.46)

DAY 5

This verse is a solemn ending to a serious passage, and underlines the gravity of what is at stake. Throughout these verses (Matt. 25:31–46), Jesus has been describing two types of people: the blessed people (v.34) and the cursed people (v.41). The blessed are those who love and serve Jesus unknowingly; the cursed are the ones who fail to discern the presence of Jesus in the suffering of His people.

In the concluding verse of this passage, these two groups of people face two distinct destinies. The blessed are granted eternal life and an inheritance in the kingdom (v.34). The cursed are judged on how they have treated the least of the brothers and sisters of Jesus, and despite their protests (v.44) their punishment is the eternal fire of hell 'prepared for the devil and his angels' (v.41).

These verses are often the battle ground for debating the duration of 'eternal' punishment. While the nature of heaven and hell is a subject worthy of the most serious discussion, it must never be at the expense of avoiding the challenge of Jesus regarding how we live our lives today. Those of us who love and follow Jesus must demonstrate a practical concern for the poor and marginalised. We must also warn those who vent their hatred on the people of God that they are accountable for their deeds and face a terrible Day of Judgment.

We heed the warning of these verses by heeding the words of Jesus to be salt and light (Matt. 5:13–16). When the salt of the gospel is rubbed into the wounds of the world, it preserves and protects a community from going rotten. When the light of the gospel shines in dark places, it both serves as a warning of danger and a guiding light to places of safety.

But our deeds of mercy must begin with our brothers and sisters in Christ. The mark of a saved person is the concern to do good to all people, but especially to those who belong to the family of believers (Gal. 6:10).

PRAYER

Lord, increase my love for those who have damaged their lives through sin and give me courage to take the light of the gospel into the darkest places of Your world. Amen.

THE STORY OF PASTOR GEORGE ORJI

George Orji could have excelled in any arena. He had
a thirst for knowledge, and had acquired a Diploma
in Ministry, an Intermediate Diploma in Laboratory
Technology, a Higher Diploma in Science Laboratory
Technology, a Diploma in Computer Application and a
Postgraduate Diploma in Theology. Secular and spiritual
avenues were open to him. However, he was totally sold
out for the Lord and chose full-time ministry. By 2009,
Pastor George was ministering at Good News Church in
Maiduguri, the capital of Borno State, north-eastern Nigeria,
where he lived with his wife Veronica and their two young
children, Berachah and Elioenal, aged four and two.

Pastor George was known for his unique and
innovative style of ministry. He was a man who crossed
denominational divides, ministering in a variety of
churches, and manifesting the unity of the Body of Christ
through his actions.

When the Islamist Boko Haram (Western Education
is Forbidden) group launched its initial attacks in Bauchi
State, central Nigeria over the weekend of 25–26 July,
Pastor George was in Plateau State, attending a summer
programme at the Evangelical Church of West Africa
(ECWA) Theological Seminary in Jos, where he was
pursuing a part-time Masters in Divinity. As the violence
spread into three other states including Borno, he became
increasingly concerned for his children and heavily
pregnant wife, who were still in Maiduguri, where Boko
Haram had its headquarters.

Pastor George immediately left for home. Upon

reaching Maiduguri, he entered what could only be described as a war zone. Boko Haram's compound in Maiduguri's Railway District was under siege from the Nigerian Army and Police Force, the Nigerian Air Force was circling overhead and bodies were beginning to pile up in the streets as it was becoming too dangerous to remove them.

Having gone home and been reassured of his family's safety, Pastor George felt compelled to check on one of his parishioners, a vulnerable widow who lived alonę in the area where fighting was fiercest. It seemed there was nothing to fear except stray bullets – after all, the army was after Boko Haram, and Boko Haram militants had assured local Christians that their fight was against a government that was allegedly oppressing their members. In reality, the Islamist militia was already destroying churches in the railway area, targeting and killing church leaders and kidnapping Christian men, women and children for use as human shields.

Pastor George Orji
Photo: Christian Solidarity Worldwide 2009

Accompanied by a member of his congregation named Emmanuel Ndah, Pastor George cautiously made his way to the widow's house, but upon arriving, found she had already left the area. As the men were about to return home, their car was hijacked by Boko Haram fighters, who forced them at gun and knifepoint to drive to the sect's railway headquarters.

Once there, the full extent of Boko Haram's targeting of Christians became clear as Pastor George discovered that he was one of around 250 Christians who had been forcibly abducted by the militants.

All over the compound there were bloody scenes of unspeakable cruelty. According to eyewitness survivors, upon arrival at the camp identified members of the security forces were immediately hacked to death with machetes, 'slaughtered as if they were not human beings'. The remaining captives were asked their names, and those that were clearly not Muslim were set aside. Women were locked in one room, while men were taken to another, where they were tightly bound.

It soon became evident that the militants were also attempting to Islamise their Christian captives forcibly. Women who refused to convert were kept on as human shields. However, men were immediately beheaded. In this oppressive and frightening atmosphere, many pretended to convert to Islam and even underwent conversion rituals. Some were released, while others were killed despite converting. Survivors say Boko Haram leader Yusuf Mohammed, who personally oversaw conversions and beheadings, would determine at random whether a hostage lived or died.

In these terrifying circumstances, Pastor George held fast to his faith, not with desperation, but with an increasing assurance and boldness. He continued to pastor anyone who needed comfort or reassurance. Several survivors drew strength from him as he ceaselessly prayed, sang and encouraged those around him to hold on to their faith regardless of the consequences. At one point, Pastor George turned to Emmanuel and uttered two phrases that were to become his epitaph, and that challenge and inspire every follower of Christ who hears them: *'If you survive, tell my brothers that I died well, and am living with Christ. And if we all die, we know that we die for the Lord.'*

Soon it was Pastor George's turn to face Yusuf Mohammed. Despite the incredibly daunting circumstances, his faith did not waiver. Like Stephen in Acts 7, Pastor George boldly and categorically refused to renounce his faith in Christ, and then, to the amazement of onlookers, began to preach to Yusuf Mohammed, calling on him to repent before it was too late. When he had finished, he began to sing and pray.

Pastor George kept singing and praying when the militants forced him to bow his head as they dragged him past their leader to an area a little way away from the camp. He continued to sing and pray until they brought a machete down on the back of his neck, severing his head from the rest of his body.

Shortly after Pastor George was murdered, government forces finally overran the Boko Haram headquarters. So many mutilated, decapitated and bloody bodies littered the compound and surrounding area that a decision was made to bury them quickly in a mass grave in order to avert the spread of disease. Days later, at a tearful memorial service held at his church, eyewitnesses queued up to relate their experiences in the Boko Haram camp and to recount the remarkable story of Pastor George Orji, a true man of God who was faithful unto death, who has received the crown of life, and whose testimony will long continue to serve as an inspiration.

WEEK SEVEN

WHAT DOES THE LORD REQUIRE OF YOU?

By Roger Forster

AUTHOR PROFILE

Roger Forster graduated from St John's College, Cambridge in mathematics and theology. After service in the Royal Air Force, he was an itinerant evangelist until 1974, when he established the Ichthus Christian Fellowship. He is Chairman of the Council for the Evangelical Alliance and a vice president of Tearfund. A founder of March for Jesus, he was on the board of the AD2000 Movement and the council of the Evangelical Missionary Alliance.

Roger is the author of several books, including *God's Strategy in Human History*, *Reason, Science and Faith*, *Explaining Fasting*, *Christianity, Evidence and Truth*, *Prayer* and *Suffering and the Love of God*.

INTRODUCTION

Over the years, I have had the privilege of writing Bible notes for many different groups. I have always enjoyed the challenge to assimilate the truth of the text and then concentrate it down to few, but significant, words. The overall discipline is good for me – a preacher not well-known for conciseness! Abraham Lincoln said words to this effect: you can preach all day with no preparation but you need to prepare all day to preach something worthwhile in ten minutes. Bible notes are like that.

So, I was pleased when CSW asked me to write notes on Micah 6:8, this verse being one of my favourites from the minor prophets. Micah 6:8 strengthens my convictions that we can only walk with God when we embrace humility as a lifestyle, while mercy or 'loyal loving-kindness' as some would translate, is the loving badge of real Christian discipleship (John 13:34–35).

Moreover, equally challenging is the need in my own life to act in a just manner, to that large number of distressed, disadvantaged, underprivileged, poor, oppressed and persecuted who are in this world: plenty of scope for justice? If the outcome of my modest notes is helping the reduction of this mass of suffering, I would be more than rewarded. Thank you for this opportunity.

THE HEAVENLY, HUMBLE HEART

BIBLE READING
Micah 6:1–8

KEY VERSE
'He has showed you, O man, what is good. And what does the LORD require of you? To act justly and to love mercy and to walk humbly with your God.' (Micah 6:8)

Micah 6:8 belongs to a remarkable revelation (6:1–8). God is seen in this passage as a prosecuting counsel bringing an indictment against Israel. The mountains, and creation itself, are called upon to be a jury in the case.

Not only does God charge His people but, amazingly, He indicts Himself: '… what have I done to you? And how have I wearied [burdened and bored] you?' God asks in His magnificent humility (v.3, NASB, my addition). This heart of God is incarnated in Jesus. Jesus' words in Matthew 11:29 are the only description of God's heart in the New Testament: '… I am gentle and humble of heart …' Like the revelation of the Lord in Micah, so Jesus adds to the appeal, standing amongst His own creatures and asking: 'Can any of you prove me guilty of sin?' (John 8:46). Jeremiah reports God as saying, 'What injustice did your fathers find in Me, That they went far from Me …?' (Jer. 2:5, NASB).

These revelations underline Micah's name, which means 'who is like God?'. Not only is this a superbly fitting name for the message of this book but it is also stamped on the first verse and repeated in the last verses (7:18–20): 'Who is a God like You …'

These Bible revelations of God's character confirm the conviction that our God is indeed unique. This humility of God makes it possible to 'walk humbly with our God', which, as Micah 6:8 tells us, is good. It is because God's goodness contains such humility that we can fellowship with Him and reproduce His humbleness.

Jesus calls us in Matthew 11:28–30 to come to Him if we have burdens, even if we think they came from Him (Micah 6:3). He promises us rest, fellowship and learning from Him daily what is good, just and loving in all the intricacies of our complex lives. In His presence is plenty of room for healing because His gentle and humble heart creates space for us rather than stifling our soul.

PRAYER
Lord of the heavenly, humble heart, teach me Your way and keep me from arrogance, pride and superiority, so bringing heaven to my neighbours.

HIS JUDGMENTS ARE TRUE AND JUST

BIBLE READING
Micah 6:1–8

KEY VERSE
'He has showed you, O man, what is good. And what does the LORD require of you? To act justly and to love mercy and to walk humbly with your God.' (Micah 6:8)

Micah 6:8 says that Israel should have acted differently because the Lord had shown them that acting justly was good.

Although all of mankind has a rough consensus concerning goodness, ultimately we need a word from the 'good' Lord Himself to strictly define what He in the end requires. This God had done in Moses' Law, the Psalms and the Prophets. Jesus came later to complete this revelation (Matt.

5:17). As we read the Bible, we will gain a more precisely defined understanding of truth and goodness.

We are to act justly. This word carries the meaning of weighing and making a decision concerning right and wrong, judging issues concerning others and ourselves, then doing the *right* thing. Some people, misunderstanding Jesus' words 'Do not judge' (Matt. 7) about criticism, refuse to come to a decision and commit themselves. They become victims of the 21st-century disease of non-commitment. Everybody is right and nobody is wrong, nor should they be confronted. Our verse shows that God expects people to make judgments concerning justice issues, and to do something about it.

Reflecting on World War II, a German pastor commented, 'The Nazis came for the Gypsies. I wasn't one and did nothing. They came for the Communists. I wasn't one and did nothing. They came for the Jews. I wasn't Jewish and did nothing. They came for me – and I could do nothing.' We must make just judgments and act.

In contrast, Hans and Sophie Scholl of the short-lived White Rose movement, were beheaded by the Nazis for seeking to alert Germans to the evils that were happening and shaming their German race. They secretly printed facts about the regime. Many said it was a waste of time. However, a few years ago in Germany, the brother and sister were voted in the top ten of significant Germans of all time, and Sophie by German women as the most notable German woman of the twentieth century.

Acting justly is good, says Micah. So must we act.

PRAYER
Lord Jesus, give us the courage to speak, act and labour for Your justice in the earth.

WEEK SEVEN

DAY 3

COVENANTED LOVE

BIBLE READING
Micah 6:1–8

KEY VERSE
'He has showed you, O man, what is good. And what does the LORD require of you? To act justly and to love mercy and to walk humbly with your God.' (Micah 6:8)

Today we look at the word translated in verse 8 as 'mercy' (the Hebrew word *hesed*), which could variously be expressed as 'loving-kindness' or 'loyalty' or even 'covenant love'. All love, by definition, contains the element of commitment found in say, a marriage covenant. However, in the light of much unfaithfulness, we often need to swear (vow) to love.

'Love is not love that alters when

it alteration finds,' says Shakespeare magnificently. God swears His covenanted love to us in the Bible. The word 'mercy' or 'covenant love' occurs six times in Hosea, and God expounds its meaning by Hosea's story. His unfaithful wife, having been used by lovers, is abandoned to the slave market. Hosea is to buy and love her back into a proper wife again, while God says of unfaithful Israel: 'I will betroth you to me for ever ... in love and compassion' (Hosea 2:19). If God's love is like that, then Hosea and anyone wanting to be God-like (Micah) must love as He. 'Be imitators of God, therefore, as dearly loved children and live a life of love, just as Christ loved us and gave himself up ... a sacrifice ...' (Eph. 5:1–2).

In pastoring young men for marriage, I have been disturbed to find a growing number of prospective husbands talk in terms like: 'How do I know I will still love her after five years?' And: 'Supposing I meet someone to whom I am more attracted?' And: 'What when she is older and not so pretty ...?'

The lack of commitment and ability to commit is less than human, let alone less than God-like. Supposing God had approached our salvation and relationship in that way? We never could have said, 'He has loved me with an everlasting love [*hesed*]' (Jer. 31:3), so being assured of everlasting life. However, 'Christ loved me and gave Himself for me', covenanting His love in the blood of commitment (see Gal. 2:20). No wonder, then, He says to us that He requires us to love loving-kindness in our dealings with Him and each other.

PRAYER
Lord, give us that love for You and each other, which tells the world we are Your disciples. (See John 13:34–35.)

THE DOWN-AND-OUT GOD

BIBLE READING
Micah 6:1–8

KEY VERSE
'He has showed you, O man, what is good. And what does the LORD require of you? To act justly and to love mercy and to walk humbly with your God.' (Micah 6:8)

I have just finished a long flight back from ministry in Nepal. I was reminded of Gandhi, the great Indian leader and admirer of Jesus, even though he never declared his exclusive commitment to our Lord. The reason I thought of him was because of the state of the cabin's toilets. I half-heartedly tried to clear up and tidy the condition they were in. Gandhi, on one state occasion, was missing until found in the toilets cleaning up the mess left by others. I, and presumably he, feel sure this is what Jesus who was 'gentle and humble of heart' would do (Matt. 11:29). I confess I was half-hearted, but it is a start!

Our Lord washed our feet, took the lowest place, touched lepers, wept publicly with the heartbroken, ran to greet prodigals, cooked and served our breakfast, sought lost sheep, walked miles and only rode once – and that was the 'colt, the foal of a donkey', not a decent stallion. (Of course, as many have said, kings did ride asses occasionally, when coming in peace, but Jesus' act was deliberately to emphasise the scripture from Zechariah 9:9–11, where it says that the people were to rejoice because their king comes justly and having salvation, gentle and riding on a donkey.) The result of such a lowly heart would be peace rather than arrogance and aggression.

Humility does not provoke aggression, neither does our humble Lord. So, to walk with a humble God requires humility, getting down to where He is to fellowship, so as to respond to the prompts of His gentle dove (Spirit) to lowly, servant-hearted acts.

It will mean a humble respect for the least of those of no status, and a sincere, not cynical, honouring of those who have status.

The higher you know that you have been lifted by Christ (see Eph. 2:6), the easier it is to stoop down to the lowly and walk with God.

Look at Jesus.

PRAYER

Jesus, let me find happiness with those poor in spirit who nevertheless have the kingdom You promised. (See Matt. 5:3.)

JUST TESTING

DAY 5

BIBLE READING
Micah 6:1–8

KEY VERSE
'He has showed you, O man, what is good. And what does the LORD require of you? To act justly and to love mercy and to walk humbly with your God.' (Micah 6:8)

A story is told of an atheist who, frustrated by the problems and pains of life, railed against God: 'God, if You are there, why don't You tell us what to do?' To his surprise, a voice boomed out of the sky: 'He has showed you, O man, what is good. And what does the LORD require of you? To act justly and to love mercy and to walk humbly with your God.' Taken aback, our friend said, 'Oh sorry, I was just testing.' 'I also,' returned the voice.

In the days of Micah, God's people were again trying God out, as we all do occasionally. 'Why should He give us such problems to cope with – poverty, hunger, war, hatreds, suffering? We can't handle these things. Life should be all sweet. We don't deserve all these pressures.' Sometimes we feel so alone, we argue, 'There is no God.' However, still, there arises that nagging within: 'You know what is right to do – feed the hungry, have compassion on the sick and dying, stand with the exploited, oppressed and marginalised.' Even atheists are better than their doctrines, thank God, and find their feelings to do good drowning their godless philosophy.

Jesus said that He desired mercy, not ritualistic sacrifices (Matt. 9:13; 12:7). These cultic practices can never replace loving-kindness, which is the Hebrew word translated 'mercy'.

The immediate context of Micah 6:8 is verses 6 and 7. There, we read of coming to God with burnt offerings, thousands of rams and ten thousand rivers of oil, even offering our firstborn as an atonement for our sin. These, though, are an insult if we are contributing to a merciless society and offering no respite to its victims. Anyway, it was God's agenda to offer His firstborn Son and pour out rivers of His anointing Spirit. He, not we, makes the inestimable sacrifice. This great act of God reaches deeper into our beings than the milk of human kindness, and releases into the world not only our activity but also His healing oil.

PRAYER

Lord, please today release Your love and Spirit's activity through my heart into the world where it belongs.

THE STORY OF FATHER GHEORGHE CALCIU-DUMITREASA

*Why do good men remain silent? We want you to feel with
us in our suffering and cry out when we cannot: 'Enough!'*

On 10 March 1979, inside Nicolae Ceaușescu's highly
repressive Romania, Orthodox priest Father Gheorghe
Calciu-Dumitreasa disappeared. Three months later his wife
learnt that he had been sentenced to ten years in prison! So,
what crime was worthy of such a long sentence?

   In 1978, Father Calciu had been dismissed from his
post of Professor for French and New Testament Studies
at the Bucharest Theological Seminary because of his
outspokenness on Christian issues. He then decided that the
youth of Bucharest needed to hear the words of Jesus, as
the only thing they had learnt was Marxism. He therefore
started a small prayer group, and before long this grew to
over one hundred young people committed to the teachings
of Jesus. During Lent 1979, he preached a series of seven
Lenten sermons entitled 'Seven Words to Romanian Youth'.
These sermons were not political calls for an uprising or any
such radical thing, but were simply the Word of God.

   The first three sermons were delivered from Father
Calciu's church pulpit, but when he came to preach the
fourth on the fourth week, he arrived at his church to
find the doors closed! So, quite simply, he preached in
the courtyard. The fifth week, the gates to the courtyard
were closed, so the spiritually hungry young people of

Bucharest climbed the walls to hear the Word of God. On finishing his seventh sermon, Father Calciu was arrested and subsequently began the ten-year sentence handed down to him.

This was not the first time that Calciu had seen the inside of a Romanian prison, as in 1948 he had been arrested along with 10,000 other students opposed to the Marxist philosophy being espoused by the newly-formed government of the day. On that occasion, he didn't leave prison until some seventeen years later, when he was released together with over one million other political prisoners; an estimated 300,000 others had already died of hunger or from torture, forced labour and despair!

On his second stretch in prison, he spent the first two years and seven months in a small isolation cell without light, heat, air or even a bed! He was given food only every third day!

Because of the words at the beginning of this story, which were written by Father Calciu prior to his arrest and

Father Gheorghe Calciu-Dumitreasa
Photo: Christian Solidarity Worldwide 2009

circulated in the West, Christians everywhere were praying and campaigning on behalf of this saintly man of God.

After his time of desperate isolation, Father Calciu was taken to share a cell with two fellow prisoners. At last he had company, and he was so grateful that he could speak to other humans, having spent the last fifteen months conversing with a friendly cockroach in his isolation cell!

It wasn't long before the two men with whom Calciu now shared a cell, told him that they had been given orders to kill him! Because of the adverse publicity from Western Christians, President Nicolae Ceauşescu wanted him killed, but it had to be in a fight with other prisoners, as he did not want the State implicated.

These two men were certainly up to the job, one was a serial killer and the other had already spent three years in prison for killing his own mother! On carrying out their task they were to be rewarded with freedom!

It wasn't long before Father Calciu realised that the conversations he had with the cockroach were much more edifying than those with these men! Daily they would taunt him with their vile and vitriolic abuse. They would kick and punch him, rip handfuls of his hair from his head, make him drink his own urine and eat his own excreta.

However, Calciu was determined nothing would get in the way of his communing with God; daily he would get on his knees to pray and cry out to God. During these times of prayer, the insults and violence would be at their worst, but Calciu would quietly continue in prayer.

However, one day when he was praying he noticed all was quiet and still. Eyes closed, he continued until he said his final amen. When he opened his eyes he saw the most astonishing sight – on either side of him were his two cell mates, kneeling in silence with tears streaming down their faces.

Through the tears they told him that they had done

everything humanly possible to break his spirit, but nothing had worked. They said that before meeting him, neither of them had known what love was, but Father Calciu's only response to their brutality was to love them! In turn, Calcui explained that it was humanly impossible for him to love them, but he was simply reflecting God's love through his life and actions. He then told them that God had so loved them that he had sent His only Son, Jesus, to die on the cross to save them from their sin. He also explained that no one was such a bad sinner that they were beyond redemption. Father Calciu simply led the two men into the kingdom of God!

The next day the men were taken from the cell and never seen again, almost certainly killed for not carrying out the orders they had been given.

Father Calciu died in 2006 in Washington DC, after a long illness. No doubt he has now been reunited in glory with his one-time tormentors!

WEEK EIGHT
BLESSED BY GOD

By Jonathan Aitken

AUTHOR PROFILE

Jonathan Aitken is an author, broadcaster, lecturer and campaigner for prison reform. He is a former Cabinet Minister, Member of Parliament and ex prisoner.

Jonathan's twelve books include biographies; two volumes of autobiography; and spiritual writings.

Jonathan is on the board of several charitable bodies including Caring for Ex-Offenders and Prison Fellowship International. He is Honorary President of Christian Solidarity Worldwide.

Jonathan is a frequent speaker at Alpha events. He says, 'Back in 1997 I must have been just about the most reluctant attendee ever at an Alpha course but it changed my life and set me on the path of spiritual discovery and Christian commitment.'

INTRODUCTION

As Honorary President of CSW, I am delighted to contribute to this book of devotions.

In my own daily prayers, I often concentrate on our brothers and sisters in Christ who are being persecuted for their faith. I have met many of them both at home and in countries overseas. I never fail to be awed and humbled by their steadfastness and courage. When praying for them, the Beatitudes from the Sermon on the Mount (Matt. 5:1–12) are a great source of inspiration. Indeed, they are a direct reminder that from the poor in spirit (v.3) to the persecuted and insulted (v.11), Jesus loves those who suffer for Him.

So, for the next five days in our prayerful readings, let us rejoice that those who are more marginalised by the world are the most blessed by God.

WEEK EIGHT

DAY 1

THE POOR IN SPIRIT

BIBLE READING
Matthew 5:1–12

KEY VERSE
'Blessed are the poor in spirit, for theirs is the kingdom of heaven. Blessed are those who mourn, for they will be comforted.' (vv.3–4)

Adversity can be the gateway to a deeper faith. The phrase 'poor in spirit', found here in our key verse for today, has a profound history in the Old Testament and refers to those who have been ground down by longstanding social and political distress yet have kept faith and confidence in God. They have learned to trust in Him completely throughout their trials and tribulations. They find to their amazing joy that the kingdom of heaven is God's free gift to them.

A similar gift can be bestowed on those who mourn. The death of a loved one is a shattering experience. Yet in the depths of such suffering, God moves closer to us than we can understand with His loving comfort. It is in such dark moments that we may discover the power of Jesus 'to bind up the broken-hearted' (Isa. 61:1).

Those who are persecuted for their faith are often 'the poor in spirit'. They suffer appalling adversities, both political and physical. Sometimes they are in mourning for loved ones whose lives have been ended by torture or acts of violence. Yet despite these horrendous losses and pressures, they remain steadfast in their faith because they put their trust in God and God alone.

Throughout these Beatitudes, and perhaps particularly with the first beatitude which opens the Sermon on the Mount, the word 'blessed' means 'made happy by God'. What a revolutionary and inspirational thought Jesus put into the hearts of His hearers, that the poor in spirit – the worst of sufferers – should be first in the kingdom of heaven.

PRAYER

Heavenly Father, we thank You for the first Beatitudes in the Sermon on the Mount and for their revolutionary message. May we follow these great teachings of Jesus by honouring the poor in spirit and comforting those who mourn. For the sake of our Lord and Saviour, Jesus Christ. Amen.

SPIRITUAL HUNGER

BIBLE READING
Matthew 5:1–12

KEY VERSE
'Blessed are those who hunger and thirst for righteousness, for they will be filled ... Blessed are the pure in heart, for they will see God.' (vv.6,8)

Spiritual fulfilment and purity of heart are two of the greatest blessings of the Christ-centred life. Jesus was talking here on a completely different level to human food, drink or carnal pleasure. He was opening the minds of His listeners to the heavenly joys of purity and the inner happiness that comes when spiritual thirst or hunger is satisfied.

It is a surprising feature of our

secular age that spiritual hunger does not appear to be diminishing. When people cease to trust in God, they believe in anything rather than nothing. Modern mysticism embraces every nonsensical nostrum from tarot cards and astrology to good luck charms worn by celebrities. We have entered a new age of worshipping idols. Yet spiritual hunger continues. It may seem old-fashioned to answer it by searching for goodness (the main meaning of 'righteousness' in this Gospel) and purity of heart. Yet, this is what Jesus was teaching us to do. He awakened in His hearers a passionate desire to be right with God.

Jesus' call can be powerful as ever today, but not many have the undivided love and loyalty to respond to it wholeheartedly. How do we satisfy our spiritual hunger and thirst? One of the earliest and wisest answers to this ancient question was given by the prophet Jeremiah: 'You will seek me and find me when you seek me with all your heart' (Jer. 29:13).

PRAYER

Heavenly Father, we cannot live by earthly bread alone. Help us to change the direction of our lives away from the transitory devices and desires of our own hearts, such as love of money, idolisation of the celebrity culture and belief in foolish superstitions. Instead, guide us towards a hunger and thirst for Your righteousness until we are blessed by the spiritual joy of seeing You. For the sake of our Lord and Saviour, Jesus Christ. Amen.

DAY 3

THE MEEK AND THE MERCIFUL

BIBLE READING
Matthew 5:1–12

KEY VERSE
'Blessed are the meek, for they will inherit the earth ... Blessed are the merciful, for they will be shown mercy.' (vv.5,7)

The meek and the merciful are two groups who win few of the world's prizes yet are profoundly happy with God in their spiritual lives.

'... the meek will inherit the land and enjoy great peace,' says the author of Psalm 37 in verses which begin with the exhortation 'Do not fret' and advise us to trust, delight and commit to the Lord (vv.1–11). Those who follow this path become so humble before God that He can exalt them without any danger of their getting self-centred and proud.

Meekness and mercifulness are natural companions in God's world. This is because those who have tasted the Lord's forgiveness and mercy know the deepest dimensions of happiness. But their joy is enhanced by respect for their divine benefactor. As the great nineteenth-century Baptist preacher C.H. Spurgeon put it, 'None fear the Lord like those who have experienced his forgiving love.'

Humility and mercy are the polar opposites of two destructive sins. The first is pride, which C.S. Lewis rightly described as 'the great sin ... the complete anti-God state of mind'. The second is 'unforgiveness', which is often accompanied by bitterness and anger. Most of us have been guilty of both these faults at moments in our lives. If we can defeat these sins and move to the God-centred life of being meek and merciful, the rewards of joy that Jesus promised will be ours.

PRAYER

Heavenly Father, help us to defeat our sinful impulses to be proud and unforgiving. May we fight off such temptations and follow the example of Your ministry, setting aside all yearnings for recognition, all desire for applause, and all tendencies to be hard and judgmental on others. Instead may we follow the teachings of Your Son, to be humble and merciful, for by this we will inherit the blessings of Your forgiveness, Your peace and Your grace. For the sake of our Lord and Saviour, Jesus Christ. Amen.

PEACE AND RECONCILIATION

DAY 4

BIBLE READING
Matthew 5:1–12

KEY VERSE
'Blessed are the peacemakers, for they will be called sons of God.' (v.9)

I once knew a remarkable and historic peacemaker. He was the thirty-seventh President of the United States, Richard Milhous Nixon. As his biographer, I praised him as the statesman who brought China into the international community; who achieved détente with a nuclear disarmament treaty with the Soviet Union; and who ended America's disastrous involvement in the Vietnam war. Nixon's inspiration for these achievements can be traced to his mother Hannah, a devout Quaker who made her son learn the Beatitudes in childhood. She taught him that to be a peacemaker was a great vocation.

For all his gifts, Nixon often did not find peace for himself. During most of his political career he was a troubled soul. This is sometimes the way of assertive leaders, including church leaders. The history of religious hostilities across the millennia reminds us that reconciliation has often been far too low on the agenda of many denominations and churches.

We are called to imitate Jesus Christ and to follow His teachings. In His Sermon on the Mount, a few verses after the Beatitudes, He told His listeners to turn the other cheek and to avoid litigation: '… if someone wants to sue you and take your tunic, let him have your cloak as well' (Matt. 5:40). It is advice powerfully amplified by St Paul, who urged the Corinthians to resolve their disputes privately between believers (1 Cor. 6:1–6). Lawsuits between Christians, of the kind that are now spreading like a virus in the Episcopal Church of the United States, must make the angels weep.

A divisive spirit saddens the Lord. Those who reconcile the estranged delight Him. In our daily devotions at the office of CSW, we frequently pray for peace. When this blessing is granted to troubled nations and peoples (look at what happened in the former Iron Curtain countries!) persecution usually ceases too. Blessed indeed are the peacemakers of our time.

PRAYER

Heavenly Father, grant us the blessing of peace in our hearts. May we also, at every opportunity, work for peace and reconciliation in the hearts of others. Amen.

WEEK EIGHT

DAY 5

PRAY FOR THE PERSECUTED

BIBLE READING
Matthew 5:1–12

KEY VERSE
'Blessed are those who are persecuted because of righteousness, for theirs is the kingdom of heaven. Blessed are you when people insult you, persecute you and falsely say all kinds of evil against you because of me.'
(vv.10–11)

Persecution of Jesus' followers has been a feature of Christian life since the days of Herod and Nero. Sadly, this abomination is even more prevalent in the twenty-first century than it was in the first century. Evil regimes such as North Korea and Burma are rightly condemned for their systematic imprisonment and torture of contemporary believers. But there are pockets of almost as bad persecution in parts of India, Pakistan, Vietnam, China and many other countries where Christian Solidarity Worldwide fulfils its mission 'to be a voice for the voiceless' by speaking out against such outrages with public advocacy to national parliaments and international assemblies across the world.

The persecuted appear to be the worst of victims and the greatest of losers. Not so. For Jesus teaches us that those who suffer for His sake gain the kingdom of heaven. Whenever I meet those who have been willing to face oppression, humiliation, harassment, imprisonment and even the threat of death for the Lord's sake, I am awed and amazed by their heroism. It is deeply moving that the Suffering Church is so different from the comfortable churches in the West.

Persecuted Christians look for our prayers not that they may have easier times but that they may be steadfast in their faith under terrible pressures. They know the joy of utter faithfulness to Jesus. At CSW, we rejoice in their strength, support them in our intercessions and give them practical backing through our advocacy.

PRAYER

Heavenly Father, comfort and strengthen all those who suffer for Your sake in the Persecuted Church. May we support those sufferers in our daily prayers. We also pray for the work of CSW, and for our mission to be a voice for the voiceless. Especially we pray for individuals, families and whole nations who are persecuted for their faith. May they continue steadfastly and courageously to bear witness to Your holy name, secure in the promise of Your Son to them, 'theirs is the kingdom of heaven'. For the sake of our Lord and Saviour, Jesus Christ. Amen.

THE STORY OF CARLOS LAMELAS

Carlos sat upright on his bed, his back against the wall, forcing his eyes to stay open. Every so often, a guard would peer through the tiny screen in the door to make sure that both prisoners in the cell were awake and sitting up. Although there was almost no room in the cell to move around, lying down and sleeping were not permitted during the day, while at night fluorescent lights were left on, full strength, making it difficult to sleep soundly.

It was May and the oppressive Caribbean heat was starting to set in. The air in the tiny cell where Carlos spent his days and nights was stagnant, as the little screen in the door provided the only source of ventilation. The trickle of water and drain in the corner was their only source of drinking water, as well as their shower and their toilet. 'Has God abandoned me?' Carlos wondered.

He had been in prison for three months. His wife, Uramis, and their two young daughters had been thrown out of their home after his arrest and virtually all of their belongings had been confiscated by government officials. They were staying in a cramped apartment with Carlos's elderly parents in a crumbling building in Old Havana. Carlos felt helpless when Uramis told him about their difficulties in making ends meet.

The Cuban government had accused Carlos of human trafficking, and thus far had not allowed him to defend himself in a trial. He knew, however, that these charges had been invented by government officials to hide the real reason behind his arrest: daring to speak out against government interference in the denomination he led. His real crime was to have called for true religious freedom in Cuba, a country where despite some freedom to worship, the government attempts to control religious groups as much as possible.

The government had first tried to silence him. They organised a new election for the presidency of the denomination, a position to which Carlos had been elected by the church leaders from across the country. The plan backfired, however, when despite intimidation the denomination unanimously voted in favour of Carlos continuing as president. That was when government officials decided to imprison the pastor and denominational leader on these false charges.

At first Carlos thought it would be a matter of days, maybe a week or two, before this mistake was cleared up and he was allowed to return to his family and his ministry. But as the weeks turned into months, he began to wonder. He knew of political dissidents and independent journalists who had been given 25-year prison sentences in a massive crackdown on human rights defenders in 2003, and he

Carlos Lamelas
Photo: Christian Solidarity Worldwide 2009

worried that he would suffer a similar fate.

'I felt like Elijah,' he said. 'I told God I had had enough. How much longer would it be?'

To his surprise, God replied! 'He told me, like He told Elijah, to get up! That my work was not done. He showed me His glory, how close He was to me, and that He would answer even my smallest prayer.' Carlos's Bible, which he was allowed to keep with him, helped to sustain him throughout his imprisonment, and with it he led his cellmate and a number of other prisoners to Christ.

Then, the letters began to arrive; from North America, Europe, even as far as Mongolia. Christians from around the world sent letters to his home and to the prison, telling him and his family that they were not forgotten.

As the letters kept coming, Carlos noticed that a particular official who had made life particularly difficult for him and even claimed to be responsible for his arrest, seemed to have disappeared. A week later, another prison guard approached him and told him where the official had gone. 'He is the only member of staff here who speaks good English. We can't give you the letters until we read them first, but so many have been arriving that he spends all day, every day reading and translating your letters. Can you tell the people to please stop writing them? We don't have the capacity to censor them all!'

Carlos replied that he was sorry, but he didn't personally know the people who were writing to him and had no idea how to contact them. He and Uramis both saw God's sense of humour in the situation and also took enormous encouragement from the amount of international support.

In June, 2006, after four months in prison, Carlos was suddenly released. The guards came to his cell to take him, he thought, to his weekly meeting with his wife. 'You're going,' they said. When he followed them he realised that they meant he was leaving the prison.

However, his release from prison did not signify the end of his ordeal. The government had not dropped the charges of human trafficking. Over the following months Carlos felt as if he was in a different kind of prison, knowing that at any moment he could be picked up again. His seven-year-old daughter was especially fearful that her father would be taken away. She refused to leave his side, accompanying him whenever he left the house.

The hot, sticky summer months went by with no word from the government. The weather grew cooler and each day Carlos wondered if it would be the day he would learn his fate. In late November his lawyer called, but not with the news he had been hoping for. The charges would not be dropped; instead he would go on trial on 20 December.

His heart sank. He spoke to Uramis, their daughters and his parents, and they prayed together. He managed to contact organisations such as Christian Solidarity Worldwide, which alerted European governments and mobilised Christians around the world to pray for him and his family.

At the beginning of December, perhaps in response to the international attention, the government unexpectedly changed his trial date. He learned that he would be tried the next day, on 4 December. The last-minute change of date made it impossible for international observers to request permission to attend the trial.

On the day of the trial, Carlos went to the court with his lawyer. Uramis went with them and sat in the visitor's section of the courtroom. The judge came and took his seat. Surprisingly, the state prosecutor did not appear.

The court waited until finally another lawyer entered the room. He informed the judge that the state prosecutor assigned to the case had fallen ill that morning and would not be able to attend. The new lawyer had been sent to take his place.

The judge agreed and asked the prosecution to start by making the government's case against Carlos. The prosecutor stood and began to speak, but instead of laying out the evidence of 'human trafficking' against Carlos, he shocked the court by stating that after reviewing the case and all the materials of the state prosecutor, he could not find any evidence whatsoever that Carlos was involved in human trafficking. He recommended that the case be thrown out and Carlos's name cleared.

The judge, Carlos and his laywer were all stunned. The judge asked the defence lawyer if he had anything to say.

'Not really,' he replied. 'The prosecution has just given my arguments!'

'Well then,' said the judge, 'if the prosecution and the defence agree that this man is innocent, I don't see that I have any choice but to drop these charges. Carlos Lamelas, you are free to go.'

The story does not end there. Carlos and his family are still in Cuba. The government continues to try to control religious expression as much as possible. They have not been permitted to return to their home or to their church and ministry. Instead, Carlos has become a pastor of pastors, discipling other church leaders and organising inter-denominational outreach events. With no legal way to make a living, the family struggles to make ends meet.

Life in Cuba is not easy for Carlos and Uramis. However, they saw God's faithfulness and power demonstrated over and over during that difficult year. They also saw the power of the united Body of Christ around the world, interceding for and encouraging them through their letters of support. As long as they remain in Cuba, although it carries risks, the family are committed to carrying on with God's work, and in particular ensuring that if any other church leader is subjected to a similar ordeal, those cases are made known to the worldwide Church as well.

CWR Trusted all over the world

CWR HAS GAINED A WORLDWIDE reputation as a centre of excellence for Bible-based training and resources. From our headquarters at Waverley Abbey House, Farnham, England, we have been serving God's people for over 40 years with a vision to help apply God's Word to everyday life and relationships. The daily devotional Every Day with Jesus is read by nearly a million readers an issue in more than 150 countries, and our unique courses in biblical studies and pastoral care are respected all over the world. Waverley Abbey House provides a conference centre in a tranquil setting.

For free brochures on our seminars and courses, conference facilities, or a catalogue of CWR resources, please contact us at the following address.
CWR, Waverley Abbey House, Waverley Lane, Farnham, Surrey GU9 8EP, UK

Telephone: **+44 (0)1252 784719**
Email: **mail@cwr.org.uk**
Website: **www.cwr.org.uk**

CWR Applying God's Word
to everyday life and relationships

Discrimination, torture, imprisonment, even death – this is the price Christians can pay for following their faith.

And it is for this reason that Christian Solidarity Worldwide exists: to address this injustice and stand in solidarity with the oppressed.

CSW is a voice for voiceless Christians by speaking on behalf of others – we ensure that the UK and US governments, the EU and UN hear the voice of the persecuted. CSW urges these governments and international bodies to take action to alleviate the suffering Christians face.

The powerful combination of prayer, lobbying and international action has changed the lives of many persecuted Christians.

Be a voice for the voiceless and you can change lives.

Website: **www.csw.org.uk**
Email: **admin@csw.org.uk**
Telephone: **0845 456 5464**

CHRISTIAN
SOLIDARITY
WORLDWIDE
VOICE FOR THE VOICELESS

National Distributors

UK: (and countries not listed below)
CWR, Waverley Abbey House, Waverley Lane, Farnham, Surrey GU9 8EP.
Tel: (01252) 784700 Outside UK (44) 1252 784700 Email: mail@cwr.org.uk

AUSTRALIA: KI Entertainment, Unit 21 317-321 Woodpark Road, Smithfield, New South Wales 2164. Tel: 1 800 850 777 Fax: 02 9604 3699 Email: sales@kientertainment.com.au

CANADA: David C Cook Distribution Canada, PO Box 98, 55 Woodslee Avenue, Paris, Ontario N3L 3E5. Tel: 1800 263 2664 Email: swansons@cook.ca

GHANA: Challenge Enterprises of Ghana, PO Box 5723, Accra. Tel: (021) 222437/223249 Fax: (021) 226227 Email: ceg@africaonline.com.gh

HONG KONG: Cross Communications Ltd, 1/F, 562A Nathan Road, Kowloon.
Tel: 2780 1188 Fax: 2770 6229 Email: cross@crosshk.com

INDIA: Crystal Communications, 10-3-18/4/1, East Marredpalli, Secunderabad – 500026, Andhra Pradesh. Tel/Fax: (040) 27737145 Email: crystal_edwj@rediffmail.com

KENYA: Keswick Books and Gifts Ltd, PO Box 10242-00400, Nairobi.
Tel: (254) 20 312639/3870125 Email: keswick@swiftkenya.com

MALAYSIA: Salvation Book Centre (M) Sdn Bhd, 23 Jalan SS 2/64, 47300 Petaling Jaya, Selangor. Tel: (03) 78766411/78766797 Fax: (03) 78757066/78756360
Email: info@salvationbookcentre.com

Canaanland, No. 25 Jalan PJU 1A/41B, NZX Commercial Centre, Ara Jaya, 47301 Petaling Jaya, Selangor. Tel: (03) 7885 0540/1/2 Fax: (03) 7885 0545 Email: info@canaanland.com.my

NEW ZEALAND: KI Entertainment, Unit 21 317-321 Woodpark Road, Smithfield, New South Wales 2164, Australia. Tel: 0 800 850 777 Fax: 02 9604 3699
Email: sales@kientertainment.com.au

NIGERIA: FBFM, Helen Baugh House, 96 St Finbarr's College Road, Akoka, Lagos.
Tel: (01) 7747429/4700218/825775/827264 Email: fbfm@hyperia.com

PHILIPPINES: OMF Literature Inc, 776 Boni Avenue, Mandaluyong City.
Tel: (02) 531 2183 Fax: (02) 531 1960 Email: gloadlaon@omflit.com

SINGAPORE: Alby Commercial Enterprises Pte Ltd, 95 Kallang Avenue #04-00, AIS Industrial Building, 339420. Tel: (65) 629 27238 Fax: (65) 629 27235 Email: marketing@alby.com.sg

SOUTH AFRICA: Struik Christian Books, 80 MacKenzie Street, PO Box 1144, Cape Town 8000. Tel: (021) 462 4360 Fax: (021) 461 3612 Email: info@struikchristianmedia.co.za

SRI LANKA: Christombu Publications (Pvt) Ltd, Bartleet House, 65 Braybrooke Place, Colombo 2. Tel: (9411) 2421073/2447665 Email: dhanad@bartleet.com

USA: David C Cook Distribution Canada, PO Box 98, 55 Woodslee Avenue, Paris, Ontario N3L 3E5, Canada. Tel: 1800 263 2664 Email: swansons@cook.ca

CWR is a Registered Charity - Number 294387
CWR is a Limited Company registered in England - Registration Number 1990308